In loving memory of a dear friend, Susie

THE BISHOP AND I

'Eileen Carey has produced a fascinating study of the joys, challenges, perils and rewards of being married to an Anglican bishop. In addition to reflecting on her own marriage, she has encouraged over twenty most remarkable episcopal spouses from all over the world to talk freely to her, and the result is a gripping, often moving panorama of the unity in diversity which is the hallmark of the Anglican Communion. This topical book will appeal to all those who are interested not just in the private life of the clergy but in the institution of marriage itself.'

Susan Howatch

'These are the stories of significant members of a remarkable global family. I have found the shadow of the Cross on many pages. I have also read something of the strength of the Resurrection in this unique collection of personal pilgrimages. I know the courage and faith told in these pages will give renewed encouragement and vision for our own journey.'

Christine Eames
World Wide President, The Mothers' Union

The Bishop and I

Taking the lid off the Church's best-kept secret

Eileen Carey

with Andrew Carey

Hodder & Stoughton
LONDON SYDNEY AUCKLAND

First published in Great Britain 1998

1 3 5 7 9 10 8 6 4 2

British Library Cataloguing in Publication
A record for this book is
available from the British Library

ISBN 0 340 65652 2

Typeset by Hewer Text Ltd, Edinburgh
Printed and bound in Great Britain by
Clays Ltd, St Ives PLC

Hodder and Stoughton Ltd
A Division of Hodder Headline PLC
338 Euston Road
London NW1 3BH

Contents

Preface

The idea for this book was conceived about three years ago. I am not a person who has always felt they had a book within them just waiting to be written. On the contrary, I am essentially a practical person, always on the move and always wanting to be 'doing'.

It was while travelling around the Anglican communion and meeting the spouses of many bishops that the urge to 'tell their story' gripped me. Their role in each province is so different, and that governs largely how it is expressed. I felt excited at the prospect of some of these stories being told and after the idea was accepted by Carolyn Armitage at Hodder, I began to plan how I would approach it.

As I lacked the confidence to go ahead on my own I asked my younger son Andrew, who is a journalist, to guide me and work with me. His help has been very significant but I take full responsibility for blemishes that remain.

I pondered long on who to ask to be contributors and in the end decided that as far as possible it should be spouses I had met on my travels, while ensuring that there was a representative from most of the provinces of the communion. There are many more stories I would have liked to tell but I had to make choices, and I am grateful to all those who agreed to contribute and therefore trusted me with their story.

Each contributor had the same questionnaire to answer and I want to thank Jennie Chesters, the contributor from England, who acted as my 'guinea pig', critically appraising all the questions and making further suggestions before it went out to all the others.

These stories are compiled from the returned questionnaires. Some of them were very full of information and others, mainly due to language difficulties, quite sparse. I have not put in anything that was not included by the contributor, although in the cases of some of those I knew well I would have loved to!

I could never have produced this book without the encouragement of my husband, who believed in me and taught me, with extreme patience, how to use a word processor on our short sabbatical leave at the beginning of 1997. So this book for me was born at Virginia Theological Seminary in the States, continued in short breaks away from Lambeth and finally completed on holiday at our flat in Bristol and at Bishopthorpe in York only six weeks later than my deadline!

I am grateful for the encouragement all my family gave me. My thanks also to Lynda Corke, my very part-time secretary, who sent out the letters and was generally the anchor at Lambeth to answer any queries from the contributors, and to Catherine Harbord, who succeeded her.

Thanks must go to Andy Day, my son-in-law, as the idea for the ring design on the cover was his.

Above all, my thanks must go to Andrew for his patience with me, all his guidance and for giving me confidence to write about colleagues who have become a very important part of my life.

I invited each contributor to offer a prayer with their story and I hope these will prove to be meaningful for the reader. They come in different forms, so please adapt them to direct your prayers for the diversity of the Anglican communion.

This book is dedicated to the memory of Susie Chang Him. She died of cancer before she could write her contribution, and her husband and twin girls did it some months after her death. It is included as the Postscript in the book.

Introduction: Eileen Carey

Fact file

Name: Eileen Carey
Date of birth: 21 November 1938
Husband: George Leonard Carey, Archbishop of
  Canterbury
Children: Rachel, born 1963; husband Andy Day
  Mark, born 1965; wife Penny
  Andrew, born 1966, wife Helen
  Elizabeth, born 1971, husband Marcus Fisher
Grandchildren: Simon, born 1986; David, born 1990;
  Jonathan, born 1994 (Day); Oliver, born 1993;
  Edward, born 1995; Emily, born 1997 (Fisher); Joseph,
  born 1996

The very last thing I would have expected to happen to me
would be to find myself, in 1991, as the wife of the new
Archbishop of Canterbury. I was born to Scottish parents of
very humble origin in a working-class town in the south-east
of England. My parents had come to find work because there
was very little in Scotland after the recession of the 1920s. My
father had been in farming as a labourer during the First
World War and had no formal training. There were many like
him unable to find work. He was taken on by a construction
firm as a general labourer and remained with them until he
had to take early retirement because of ill health in 1964.

My mother did not go out to work because she thought it was very important to be at home for me and my sister, Evelyn, three years older than me. Although there was very little money there was plenty of love in our family. My mother had a wonderful Christian faith and my sister and I went to church with her every Sunday evening and were taken to Sunday School in the afternoon. My father didn't go with us except at Christmas and Easter until I was in my early teens but then he began and was confirmed the year before I was. I was too young to question what had brought about this change of heart. It was obviously a very real experience for him and made a great difference to the quality of our family life, because we then worshipped together as a family.

I was very influenced by the wonderful American evangelist Billy Graham when he was in England in 1954 and 1956. I made a personal commitment to God which has been the great influence in my life ever since.

I met my future husband, George Leonard Carey, at a New Year party in the local church. He had just been demobbed after two years of National Service in the Royal Air Force and was back at his civilian job with the London Electricity Board in London. During his time in Iraq he had felt the call to ordination in the Anglican Church and began to pursue this calling.

Meanwhile we became engaged in June 1957 and I commenced my nursing training in London in September of that same year. George was accepted for training in the ordained ministry and in September 1958 began a four-year degree course at the London College of Divinity in north London. We got married in June 1960, halfway through his training and just before my State Final examinations. On getting my qualifications I commenced a course in radiotherapy in a hospital near the college where my husband was studying and near our first home. I earned enough to pay the bills and we looked forward to the birth of our first child in March 1962.

However, something went drastically wrong, and the day after Mothering Sunday I gave birth to a stillborn baby boy weighing 7 lb 13 oz. It was a terrible tragedy to face. We were both young and getting ready to start our work in a parish in an inner-city deprived part of London, and it was very hard to face this tragic loss and look ahead to the future. With the support of family and friends and above all the grace and comfort of our Lord Jesus Christ we slowly began to move forward.

We spent four very happy years in that first parish. During that time our next child, Rachel, was born, not without much anxiety but with excellent care by the nurses and doctors of University College Hospital. She was delivered by caesarean section on 30 May 1963 – truly a gift from God. Mark was born twenty months later and Andrew just one year after that. Our quiver was now full but we still remember, on 2 April each year, the tragic loss of our firstborn son.

From our first parish we went to Oakhill Theological College, where George taught for four years, and from there to St John's College, newly sited in Nottingham, under the leadership of Michael Green. Michael and his wife Rosemary had been a tremendous support to us when we were coping with that tragic loss eight years previously.

Both at Oakhill and at St John's College I was very involved in caring for the wives and families, and in turn that gave me many friends and wonderful support, particularly when our younger daughter was born in 1971. We now had a perfect family of two girls and two boys. Although it was very hard work bringing up four lively youngsters they have enriched our lives beyond measure and in adulthood are truly our great friends.

After five years in Nottingham we felt ready to move and were very anxious to go back to parish life. For us that is the front line of ministry. For long enough we felt we had been in the back room and needed to get back to doing theology, not just teaching it!

We moved to Durham in the north-east of England in the summer of 1975, to the parish of St Nicholas, and were to stay seven years. It was the longest we had ever stayed anywhere since we had both left home at the age of eighteen.

Much happened in our time there. We saw renewal in the church life and the lives of many people being changed by the Holy Spirit and their faith deepened, which had a great effect on us also. It was a wonderful environment for our children and gave them a firm basis of faith as the older three were in their teen years and would be flying the nest very soon.

In our sixth year my husband was asked to go for interview in Bristol to be Principal of Trinity Theological College. We felt so sure that it was not right that I did not even go with him, but when I saw his face as he got off the train I knew he had been offered the job. We were both shattered. God had called us to Durham and the work there was not finished. I felt angry with God. The church was still unfinished after massive renovations and we were worshipping in the town hall. We had grown together as a congregation, and just as we were preparing to go back into the beautifully renovated church we were being asked to go to another very tough situation. We would not be there to fulfil the vision that had been given to us as a congregation.

However, God is very gentle with His rebellious children, and we were able to stay to see the congregation back into the church with a week of celebrations before preparing for our move to the West Country and to a new work.

For the first time in our married life we found ourselves living in a house away from the college community and therefore I was not closely in touch with the work of my husband. Rachel had left home to go to college, Mark and Andrew would shortly be doing so and only Lizzie was left at home. Instead of being at the centre of the work and family, I found myself bereft of a wonderful church family in Durham, the children were mostly away from home and no longer was I fully part of the life of the college. It was strange, but an opportunity to find new direction in my life if I stopped feeling sorry for myself!

I became very involved in the local church and was elected on to the parochial church council and the pastoral committee. I met with a small group of women every Monday afternoon to study and pray together and they have continued to support me in my ministry ever since. I still got to know and supported the students and their families, but the biggest change of all was to go back to nursing after twenty-two years out of the field and away from paid employment! It was only part-time but it was wonderful to be back doing what I had been called to as a young person. I think the family felt rather proud of me.

We made many friends in Bristol, keep in touch with them and expect to retire there when the time comes.

Towards the end of our fourth year a letter arrived from the Prime Minister, offering George the position of Bishop of Bath and Wells. It was like a bolt from the blue because in our Church you have no idea that your name is even being considered. We were on the move once again! This time to a palace – the only moated bishop's palace in the country. What a contrast from our humble beginnings in Dagenham on the east side of London! Sadly our parents were no longer alive to rejoice with us and to thank God for this new opportunity He was giving us.

On 3 December 1987 my husband was consecrated in Southwark Cathedral and we started a new ministry. We very quickly felt at ease and settled in the diocese, and enjoyed the great breadth of the work. The senior staff team worked well together and we became good friends. After the first year I went back to nursing for one night shift a week and enjoyed being part of the wider community again. Life was very full indeed for us both, and Lizzie, much to my delight, was training to be a nurse in London.

Just before the appointment to Bath and Wells we had an opportunity to visit New Zealand to speak for Anglican Renewal Ministries, and decided to go round the world, as we would never have the opportunity again! Little did we know what lay ahead of us. We visited Hong Kong and then went on to Melbourne for some speaking engagements and to renew our friendship with Graeme and Caroline Rutherford and their family who had been on the staff of St Nicholas, Durham, with us. Sydney was next, to spend some time with a Marist Brother who had been on sabbatical with us in Tantur, Jerusalem, the previous year. Then the real work began in New Zealand for five weeks.

We flew into Auckland and from there to Kaitia in the north of North Island to speak. By road or air we covered the country north, south, east and west, never staying longer than a couple of nights in any one place and finally finishing in Dunedin in the south-east of South Island. We were exhausted and ready to start our return journey with a few days in Honolulu, then Vancouver and finally Toronto to spend some time with my sister and her family. We enjoyed the different cultures we found ourselves in and the joy of worshipping with congregations in many parts of the Anglican communion and feeling at one with them. We were away for about nine weeks in all and were very ready to get back to the family. We had missed them, especially as by then we had our first grandchild and wanted to enjoy watching him growing up.

Happily settled in Wells until retirement – so we thought! There was much to challenge and stimulate us. Archbishop Robert Runcie had announced his retirement and there was much speculation about his successor, by the journalists and the Church alike. We, like others, were very interested to know who would be George's 'boss' and would take the Church of England into the twenty-first century.

It was not an enviable task. Thankfully, as my husband had only been in Bath and Wells diocese for two years and was a very junior bishop, we knew that he was not in the running and that the mantle would fall on the shoulders of a senior colleague, to whom we would gladly give our full support. The speculation rolled on and on and there was the general feeling that it would be better for the Church when the announcement had been made. With the Church of England system of appointments no one knew even when the Crown Appointments Commission was meeting, as it is done in total secrecy. In the middle of July, just before our holidays, a shock high on the Richter scale hit us when an envelope was handed to my husband by the Prime Minister's appointments secretary. It contained a letter inviting him to become the 103rd Archbishop of Canterbury.

From that moment our life was changed. Although George had an overview of the work in a diocese, he had no real concept of the amount of work and the number of jobs the Archbishop of Canterbury held. Within six days of that letter arriving there was to be a press conference at Lambeth Palace to announce it to the world. Meanwhile George had been away on one of his teaching missions in the diocese, and had to leave me to convey his answer to 10 Downing Street. We were allowed to talk to no one about this, not even the family, for fear of leakage to the press. We were not even together but only had contact by phone. By the evening of the day the letter had arrived the decision had to be made. Although we discussed it, I wanted no part in the final answer because George had to be sure that God was calling him to it. As in the past, I would go with him, although this time I was terrified of the unknown!

I conveyed to the Prime Minister's secretary that evening that the answer was 'yes'. I found it very difficult to think of anything else that weekend and went around making all the necessary arrangements in a daze. I joined George for the final service of the mission in Midsomer Norton on Sunday evening and then we travelled to London to stay with our son Andrew, in order to be in good time to meet the Prime Minister the next morning.

I marvel that Andrew did not ask why we were in London; you will remember that we had been asked not to talk to anyone about it. He was so used to us using the spare bed that he did not question the reason for this particular overnight stay. After our time with the Right Honourable Margaret Thatcher all the final arrangements were made for the press conference on Wednesday morning at 11 o'clock. That evening, over a meal, we told Andrew and his wife and Liz, who happened to be off duty that evening from her hospital, and phoned Mark and Penny in Bristol and Rachel and Andy in Swindon. Their first reaction was one of disbelief and then it changed to bemusement, then horror. Even with their lack of knowledge of the enormity of the task they sensed the change it would be for us, not realising at the time that it would affect them as much as it has done. Overnight we were to become a very public family.

For normality we went back to Wells to honour commitments the next day, and returned to London on Tuesday night having shared the news of the impending announcement with all the senior staff team and our trusted secretaries. They also were dumbfounded at the suddenness and astonished at both the secrecy that had been maintained and our ability to act normally under the extreme circumstances!

All our family were able to be at the press conference to support us, including our two grandchildren, Simon who was three and David who was four months. We were totally unprepared for the tremendous amount of interest in this appointment and it began to dawn on us gradually how this was going to affect our lives. We were public property from that moment.

Life in Wells also changed. The palace office received bags of congratulatory mail every day and we were swamped by it. Photographers and journalists followed my husband as he tried to continue his engagements in the diocese. It would be about six months before we were to move to Lambeth Palace and life in our present diocese had to continue. Bath and Wells had to face a further change of leadership long before they expected to, and too much disruption was unsettling. We had our third and last Christmas in that lovely palace in Wells and then we moved to London – back to our roots, in fact.

Life has been very different for me since then. I worked my last shift as a nurse from 9 p.m. on 31 December 1990 and finished it on 1 January 1991 at 8 a.m. My career as a nurse was over! I have been asked many times whether I miss it. I miss those I cared for, but many other opportunities have been part of the new role and I have been able to use the skills I gained as a nurse in an abundance of other ways. After all, I was getting rather old to be doing all the heavy lifting that came my way as night sister with the elderly.

I have found myself so often now working from a position of weakness and lack of knowledge but finding in all that uncertainty that God's grace is more than sufficient and gets me through the toughest situations.

One of the most difficult areas to come to terms with was being stripped of what I was good at and enjoyed enormously. I had always done all my own shopping, preparing of meals, baking, dinner parties and lots of other entertaining, and I was now entering an almost unknown world of managing staff to do these things. If I was to support George in the way we saw the ministry

I was just not able to do it any other way. The many engagements that I accompany him on make any other model impossible. We still do a lot of entertaining but it is usually on a large scale and in the state rooms of the palace, and therefore apart from arranging the menus with Julie and Nick, who do the cooking, I only have to be there to host the function with George. I like nothing better than a weekend at Lambeth on our own with no staff around, preparing together simple meals which we eat from a tray on our laps and perhaps watching something on television. That doesn't happen very often unfortunately!

One of the most wonderful aspects of the work is the travel to many of the countries where there are Anglican congregations and to feel immediately at home with them. Even when there is a language difference the Anglican identity makes us feel part of a very large and intimate family. We can share their joys and their sorrows and enter into the life and culture of the country. What a privilege that is for us.

Many parts of this communion are hurting. I remember particularly the genocide in Rwanda in 1994 and our visit to be alongside the sorrowing Christians. No one there escaped the killing of at least one member of their family, and many have lost more. We saw the bodies of some of those slain still lying in the exact position to remind the world of what human can do to human and somehow try to justify the action. What about the forgotten people of Sudan, in a country still torn apart by war after over thirty years? We have visited both the south and the north and have seen what life is like for the displaced. They are constantly being moved further and further from their homes, either by the fighting getting closer in the south or by the government in the north pushing the refugee camps away from the towns and cities.

Whether on the continents of Africa, Asia, the Middle

East, North America or Europe, we come back stimulated and refreshed by our travels, having gained far more from the people we have met than we are ever able to give them.

Another important part of the work is what we do in our own diocese of Canterbury. That is where I try to give some hands-on support to a few projects. Because of my professional background in nursing I am particularly interested in the charities which care for people. I am very careful that I do not take on any more than those to which I can actually give some quality time. These have given me contact with a special care baby unit and a house in the grounds of the hospital for the parents and siblings of the children and babies seriously ill in the wards. It gives them a homely base at an extremely worrying time. I have close links with the homeless, those with psychiatric problems and a project helping with drug addiction, and have been chairperson of several church projects. I have always made sure that I am involved in no more than one of these at a time in order to give as much as possible in both time and effort. I would love to do more as I enjoy being with people.

I have found my ecumenical vision enlarged immeasurably and have for the first time taken seriously Christ's command to us, 'to be one'. The Ecumenical Patriarch from Istanbul, the Georgian Patriarch and the Russian Patriarch have visited Lambeth and Canterbury, and we have visited them and also several others.

We have been to Rome twice and I found Pope John Paul II a delightfully charismatic figure. What a wonderful richness there is in all these churches, but so much division which does not help the mission of the Church 'to preach the gospel to all people'.

I have been amazed by the amount of post I receive personally, much of it from people I don't know. Some letters are to try and reach my husband through me. Some are very critical of him, but they are in the minority. The vast majority are friendly letters, many of them wanting me to do various engagements, and they could be from anywhere in the world. Most of these have to be rejected because of an already overloaded diary. Every letter is answered and that puts tremendous pressure on me. I have had only very part-time secretarial help and the burden of all the post has been sometimes almost unbearable. Again I have had to work from a position of weakness and do something which I don't particularly enjoy, when I would rather be with people doing something active. What never ceases to amaze me is God's patience with His reluctant children, and I know I am one of the worst.

I am impatient now with telling *my* story and I want to tell the stories of some of the wonderful spouses from different parts of the Anglican communion. I will finish by just telling you that I am glad I am the wife of a clergyman. I could not have been happier in any other role. Even where I am now I know it is where God wants me and if I am obedient He can use me. For that I am daily thankful.

Patricia Bays – Canada

Fact file

Name: Patricia Bays
Date of birth: 23 November 1941
Husband: Eric Bays, Bishop of Qu'Appelle, Canada
Children: Jonathan, 28; Rebecca, 27

The diocese of Qu'Appelle is in the south-west of Canada and is part of the vast wheat-growing area. We have not yet visited that diocese, but were on holiday near Calgary in 1996 and experienced something of the immense distances between small rural communities and towns and big cities.

George and I have been to Canada many times as my only sister and her family live there, and we have also made one official visit to the east side of Canada. Yet it was in Singapore that we met Eric and Patricia! We were all there to support the bishops and people of West Malaysia, Kuching, Sabah and Singapore, as this whole region was being inaugurated into a new province of South East Asia. Moses Tay, the Bishop of Singapore, was to become the first archbishop of the new province in a magnificent service which included the legal handing over of authority from the Archbishop of Canterbury to the newly formed province. Patricia and Eric were representing Canada at the ceremony.

Patricia's life has been very different to many of the stories told in this book and she is perhaps ahead of her time. She has struggled to balance her calling as a professional Christian worker with the demands of being a clergy spouse. It is all the more impressive, therefore, to see how she has been able to give so much to the Church independently of her husband.

Patricia Bays

'I think that his ministry has limited the kind of career that I might have had in the Church,' admits Patricia honestly. 'In the places that we have lived, there has not been much opportunity for paid employment for me as a professional lay church worker.'

Before she married Eric, she had definite plans to gain some practical experience in a parish and then complete some graduate work in theology with a view to becoming a theological seminary teacher. 'Marriage to a parish priest and a life away from major training centres changed that plan, although I have been able to do some seminary teaching,' she adds.

'In my knowledge of Canadian bishops' wives, it seems to me that career questions have been the most difficult for those wives who are trained for professional ministry in the Church. Wives who are teachers or nurses seem to be able to make decisions about whether and how much they will work at their own profession,' she continues. 'But those wives who are professional church workers or are clergy have found it very difficult to get paid employment, particularly in the smaller dioceses. The kind of job for which they are trained is unlikely to be given to the bishop's wife!'

Patricia was the eldest child of a Scottish Presbyterian mother and an Irish Roman Catholic father. She was baptised and raised in the Roman Catholic Church. She grew up in a very observant family, attending Mass every Sunday, saying the family rosary, fasting on Fridays, going to church schools.

The family was part of a small Roman Catholic enclave in a predominantly Protestant area of Canada, and consequently felt themselves to be part of a minority, preserving their 'specialness' by the faithful observance of traditions. 'In church, I felt a strong sense of belonging and security, and a deep enjoyment of the mystery of worship,' she declares.

Patricia's Presbyterian grandmother lived with the family. She demanded strict standards of behaviour – in Patricia's words, 'no noisy games on Sunday'. But she also gave the children a diet of Bible stories and hymns. The notion of God as a very strict parent, 'a notion that I have had to struggle to overcome', struck home to the young Patricia.

She and her sister attended a church school, the Ontario Ladies' College. She believes that the school was one of the most formative influences on her life, in terms of academic scholarship and musical training and in her religious pilgrimage. Nevertheless, the fact that the two girls attended this school had its cost for her mother, who was refused communion in the Roman Catholic church as a result. So she decided to attend the Anglican church, seeing it as a middle way.

'I was immediately drawn to the music of the liturgy and to the prospect of singing in the choir. I taught Sunday School and was a member of the Girls' Auxiliary. This was a parish where we felt welcomed and needed. If we were not there, we were missed. The church was in the evangelical tradition with the Holy Communion celebrated at the "north" end of the Holy Table.'

When Patricia finished school she enrolled in Trinity College, an Anglican college at the University of Toronto.

Here she found a different Anglican world. The prayer-book liturgy was the same, but the liturgical customs were very different. 'The priest wore coloured vestments, people genuflected, made the sign of the cross, went to confession and went on retreats. It was here that the many parts of my earlier religious experience began to come together, the love of ritual and colour and mystery of my early Roman Catholic days, and the hymns and Scripture and active involvement of my more recent Anglican experience.'

Patricia studied English literature at Trinity College, and describes fiction, poetry and drama as ways in which she came to know God and to reflect on the great questions of life. Shortly after finishing her degree she decided to study theology. At that time there was no prospect of the ordination of women, but she was drawn to theology by natural fascination. It was an exciting time, she remembers. There were new trends in liturgy, new approaches to pastoral theology and a number of great developments in ecumenical dialogue. When she graduated she found herself moving two thousand miles away to work as a director of Christian education in a parish in Winnipeg.

It was here in 1966 that she met Eric. She worked in St George's Church and he was rector of a nearby church. Eric had been a priest for six years. He had recently returned to Canada following a year in England where he tried his vocation at the Community of the Resurrection at Mirfield. They were drawn together when asked to lead a workshop for Sunday School teachers. 'So I tell people that we met at a Sunday School teachers' meeting. It sounds so Victorian,' Patricia says.

'As Eric had already been a priest for six years when we met, I was not part of his life at the time he was making that kind of decision around his vocation. Nor was I part of his life when he was a curate or when he was working in small rural parishes. We have been in only three situations, all of them in the city: eight years in a downtown parish in Winnipeg, ten years at the theological college in Saskatoon, and now ten years in Regina where Eric has been the bishop.'

When they married, Patricia believed that her own seminary training and experience of parish work would make her very understanding of the demands of parish life. From the vantage point of experience, she admits that maybe it didn't. 'I don't think that there is a real way of preparing for the demands of life in a clergy family. You just have to adapt as you go along.'

Early on in their marriage, Patricia realised that things would work best if she exercised her ministry in areas other than those of her husband. When Eric was a parish priest, she became a member of various diocesan committees, mostly concerned with education or ecumenism. Later, she became involved in the national committee structure of the Anglican Church of Canada. In fact she served for about twenty-five years on national committees on a variety of subjects from ecumenism to world mission to doctrine. From 1992 she was the chair of the National Doctrine and Worship Committee. 'I was told that I was the first non-bishop to serve in this capacity in the Anglican communion.'

In addition, Patricia took on an international role, serving as a lay member for Canada on the Anglican Consultative Council and even chairing the ecumenism section of the Council at its 1984 and 1987 meetings. She served on the Standing Committee and Finance Committee. 'I love committee work,' she says, 'and have found this aspect of my own ministry to be very rewarding. Being on national and international committees has given me an opportunity to use my gifts outside the diocese and so not be in competition with my husband.'

Patricia has also thrown herself into the world of writing and editing. For three years she edited a church school curriculum. Later she wrote a book explaining Anglican theology and customs for lay people. She has also edited a series of stories written by Canadian women priests about their ministry.

In 1992, Patricia was awarded the Anglican Order of Merit, a special medal which recognises lay people who have contributed to the life of the Church on the national or international level.

Despite all the work Patricia has been able to do during a busy life, she nevertheless believes that her main job is to support Eric in his work. 'The role of a bishop is a difficult one and part of my job is to help things to go smoothly at home. I have chosen to travel with Eric most Sundays when he goes to the country.'

The diocese covers a vast area – 190,000 square kilometres – so there is a great deal of driving to reach the parishes. She generally drives on the way to the church and Eric drives home. 'I feel now that I know many people in the diocese. When Eric first became bishop in 1986, I used to dread the "coffee hour" after church in some parishes, as people were too shy to approach a stranger. Now I feel more at home.'

In 1993, the whole family experienced a major crisis. Eric had a heart attack and coronary surgery (a triple bypass). 'Eric's heart disease seemed to come out of the blue and caused a radical change in our lives. We had to change our diet and lifestyle. Eric spent many months off work. We had to face for the first time the threat of illness and death. We felt ourselves to be wonderfully supported by the staff of the diocese and by all the people in its parishes. We try to keep a more sensible pace of life – not always easy for a bishop – and enjoy the time that we have,' Patricia says.

Patricia Bays – Canada

Patricia's prayer

Loving God, you have created us in your image and redeemed us by your power. Strengthen all of us, clergy and lay, in the diocese of Qu'Appelle, in the ministries to which you have called us. You give us the changing seasons, the cold of winter and the heat of the sun in summer. Grant that, in all the changes of our lives, we may rest in your unchanging love.

Through Jesus Christ our Lord,

Amen

Jennie Chesters – England

Fact file

Name: Jennie Chesters
Date of birth: 11 January 1934
Husband: Alan David Chesters, Bishop of Blackburn,
England
Children: David, 20

I first became acquainted with Jennie when my husband
was vicar of St Nicholas' Church, Durham, and Alan,
Jennie's husband, was vicar of Brancepeth and Director
of Education for the diocese. We immediately clicked with
them both and enjoyed the (alas) all too few opportunities
to mix socially with them. Indeed, we only found our paths
crossing again when Alan was made Bishop of Blackburn
in 1989, after in 1987 my husband had become Bishop of
Bath and Wells.

My most amusing memory of meeting Jennie again is of
September 1992. By then my husband was Archbishop of
Canterbury and he had been invited by Alan to give a major
address at the Preston Guild Week, which is only celebrated
every twenty years. We had been in Taizé in southern France
just before the engagement, leading a thousand young people
from the Church of England on a pilgrimage, and had to fly
from Geneva to Manchester, staying the night with Alan
and Jennie to attend the function the next day.

The north of England weather ran true to form. We awoke the next day to pouring rain and low temperatures for the service, which was to be held in an enormous park in Preston with only those conducting the service under cover. The many thousands therefore had to endure torrential rain – and that included Jennie and me!

I need to add that there is a great tradition in the north of England to 'dress up' in one's best clothes and wear a hat for a celebration like this.

We stoically took our seats in the front row where, holding up our umbrellas, we attempted to juggle with service sheets, stand up and sit down at the appropriate times and look as if we were enjoying ourselves. The service was wonderful, with the music led by Graham Kendrick, a very fine song and hymn writer. He encouraged us to stand to sing, but when we did the pouring rain made a puddle in our seats and we then had to sit in it! Eventually we remained seated against his instructions.

By the end of the service not a stitch of our clothing was dry and we were due to go out to tea and for an evening service. Jennie and I made the decision to go to her house and dry our clothes, ready to join our husbands at the service in the evening. Having been in France I had no other 'Sunday best' clothes, so everything I was wearing went in to the tumble drier with a fervent prayer that the suit would not shrink.

We did not get pneumonia from this experience but could so easily have done. Whenever Jennie and I meet we have a laugh about this memorable occasion and marvel that in a country with such unpredictable weather, many events are outside because they always have been and therefore always will be!

Jennie Chesters

Jennie vowed to herself never to marry a priest. She had always been a committed churchgoer, brought up by her grandparents in Sunderland. As a young adult she continued to take part in church activities, getting to know a number of clergy families during her teaching career. She recalls, 'I fully realised many of the problems they faced. I married Alan knowing he was totally committed to his calling as a priest, which he had had since the age of only fourteen.'

And so it is one of the ironies of their life together that she now finds herself married to the Bishop of Blackburn. They were both in their thirties when they met. Jennie was already well on the way to carving out what was to be a highly successful teaching career, which included four headships of primary schools and a lectureship in religious education at Sunderland Polytechnic. Alan came to the diocese of Durham, after serving ten years in the priesthood already, as the diocesan Director of Education, taking responsibility for the policy and management of Durham's church schools. It was inevitable that their paths should cross.

'Bishop Ian Ramsey appointed him, and Bishop Ramsey had, a short time previously, asked me to serve on various diocesan education committees, including being a governor of St Hilda's College. We therefore met from time to time – not least at a committee working towards the amalgamation of St Hilda's College and St Bede's College, where he was a governor.

'It was hardly a copybook romance, but a sound foundation for two people in their late thirties,' she laughs. They began to meet at weekends in Northumberland. As reasonably well-known local public figures they managed the amazing feat of keeping their growing relationship a secret. They were engaged in 1974 and married a year later, in July 1975, after Alan had been appointed Canon of Durham Cathedral.

'The last twenty years have been action-packed and painful at times, but mostly joyful and never boring!' she declares.

It was a loving and caring Christian childhood that prepared Jennie for the two vocations that have dominated her life. Her mother and father, an accountant in the city of London, were both twenty-seven years old when Jennie, their only child, was born. Tragically, her mother died within days of puerperal fever and her father was not expected to cope with a baby. So the maternal grandparents took the young child to their Sunderland home where she was later adopted by them.

Her grandparents were heavily involved in the famous evangelical parish of All Saints, Monkwearmouth, in Sunderland. The lives of the whole family revolved around the church, prayer and Bible study. She remembers that the town of Sunderland with its proud shipbuilding history was a magnet for German bombs during the Second World War. But although their home was badly damaged her predominant memories are of a 'secure and loving childhood'.

'I belonged to many church children's organisations and we held open house to people in need, whether churchgoers or not. I can never remember a time when I did not know, and love, the second part of the General Thanksgiving, beginning "We bless Thee . . ." It was thought of as a five-finger exercise: creation, preservation, redemption, the means of grace and the hope of glory – doctrine at my grandmother's knee,' she remembers. And as Jennie grew older she learned much of the beautiful language of the Book of Common Prayer and the Authorised Version of the Bible.

This spirituality has stayed with her through the trials

and joys of adult life as well. Her top priority in every day is a period of silence for prayer, for Bible reading and for self-assessment. She still keeps the pattern she learned in her teens: adoration, contrition, thanksgiving and supplication for others as well as for herself. This ACTS eventually became PACTS, to include pausing in silence before going through the previous twenty-four hours. And in addition to PACTS, Jennie has also tried hard to use a spiritual journal to help her grow in prayer. She finds today that she can see a golden thread running through her experiences which only makes sense to her when, in her words, 'taken in conjunction with the Bible, the Sacraments and a sense of Christian history in all its successes and failures'.

When the teenage rebellion came along it was not so much against Christianity, nor even an outright rejection of her evangelical inheritance, but a gradual discovery and appreciation of other Anglican forms of worship. 'While still appreciating my evangelical background, which gave me a wonderful foundation, my love of music, colour and symbolism led me to the liturgy of the Prayer Book Catholic tradition.'

Leaving Sunderland to study in Durham was her means of escape, and she visited many churches and chapels while she was there. Further opportunities to enjoy the Church of England in all its fullness came when she finished teacher training and the family moved house. 'I later visited the whole spectrum of Anglican worship, first as an archdeacon's wife and later as the wife of a diocesan bishop. I rejoice in the diversity and see it as an enormous strength of the Church of England.'

So it was with a mature faith that she entered into the very different life of a clergyman's wife. 'We both regard marriage as lifelong and sacramental. I see my role as remaining my true self while supporting him in his calling, as he has fully supported me in my Christian vocation as a teacher. And together in family life, creating a home not only for ourselves and our son, David, but for others also.'

Alan and Jennie's life together is a partnership. They have both viewed the other's vocation as an extra dimension during the past twenty years. But Jennie does not deny that there have been the inevitable difficulties. Clergy, for example, seem to move around more often than people in other jobs. She remembers the time when Alan was appointed Archdeacon of Halifax as particularly heart-rending. She had to leave her teaching post, and to make it worse two close family members died at the same time. 'So it proved to be a quadruple bereavement and a trauma on the Richter scale,' she says.

But even this was not to blunt her enviable ability to pick herself up and move on. 'Looking back, this was counterbalanced by the friendship and support of so many Christians in so many places; I would not have had it otherwise. In retrospect God is good.'

These words of optimism are characteristic of Jennie's approach to life. She remembers being groomed by her grammar school at the age of eighteen for entry to one of England's best universities. Her ambition was to become a social worker, in this country first and then overseas. But her grandfather became ill and she felt that a four-year course was impossible. So she went to a teacher training college for two years instead, vowing that somehow, somewhere, she would get her degree. This disappointment which thwarted her early ambition instead opened up a whole new area of interest. She found primary education to be not a second best but an absorbing vocation. 'Crisis became opportunity,' she says. Incidentally, she managed to get her degree later in life with the Open University, when she was in her forties!

Similarly her desire to go overseas was also met in a rather strange way, according to God's own impeccable sense of timing. She spent four hardworking but fascinating years as head of a school in Dewsbury, Yorkshire, when Alan was Archdeacon of Halifax. The pupils were all Asian and all Muslim. 'At college I had hoped to teach Indian or Pakistani children as a missionary; now, thirty years later, I was teaching them in Yorkshire,' she laughs.

But her teaching career had already come to a close when Alan was appointed Bishop of Blackburn in 1988. She describes this as a 'God-incidence' rather than a coincidence. They decided that Jennie would take early retirement in the summer, at the final opportunity offered by the education authority. But the retirement was delayed by a term at the request of the authority, so she retired at Christmas instead. Two days later, they received the letter from Downing Street inviting Alan to be Bishop of Blackburn.

Teaching was the ideal preparation for a bishop's wife. 'Twenty-five years of teaching, lecturing in RE as a tutor in teacher education, honed my skills as a voluntary Christian communicator in parish, deanery and diocesan life. After an immensely satisfying career in school and college I now frequently speak to Christian groups, at meetings, conferences and quiet days. My career and ministry as a lay speaker on Christian topics are inextricably intertwined, and by God's grace I have been given time to use these God-given skills in the service of the diocese and beyond in a voluntary capacity,' she says.

Jennie recalls a wonderful description of the role of a bishop's wife given by a shrewd mayoress at their first civic reception after arriving at Blackburn. 'She laughingly defined my role as being a "perennial, ecclesiastical mayoress".'

Such a designation has not prevented Jennie from carving out her own role at Bishop's House. She believed that her first and continuing role was to be a wife, mother and homemaker. Like her grandmother before her, she

Galatians 3:26–28; 4:4–7 (NRSV)

Together in Christ

In Christ Jesus you are all children of God through faith. As many of you as were baptized into Christ have clothed yourselves with Christ. There is no longer Jew or Greek, there is no longer slave or free, there is no longer male and female; for all of you are one in Christ Jesus... When the fullness of time had come, God sent his Son, born of a woman, born under the law, in order to redeem those who were under the law, so that we might receive adoption as children. And because you are children, God has sent the Spirit of his Son into our hearts, crying 'Abba! Father!' So you are no longer a slave but a child, and if a child then also an heir, through God.

he annual Women's World Day of ayer, held since 1887, uses a liturgy at is written by the women of one of e participating countries; this year it from Indonesia. The form of service circulated and translated so that omen throughout the world join gether in prayer and worship. day's theme is 'Young woman, rise.' omen young and old are called to se to new life in Christ.

Our reading, chosen for today, lebrates the universality of God's mily. That is one of the things that ost excites me as I have the privilege travelling to various corners of the arth (where I often meet readers of ew Daylight). Until Jesus came, orn of a woman,' the Jews saw emselves as God's exclusive, special ple. When Jesus came as a Jew, n under the law,' it was to bring mption and freedom to Jew and

Gentile alike. Paul was writing to Christians who were being persuaded that they needed to continue to live under Jewish religious rules. 'No way!' he says. Whatever our ethnic or religious background, whatever our social status, whatever our gender, we are adopted into God's family and can have the confidence to call God 'Father'. We can even use the same familiar name, 'Abba', that Jesus used. That is special.

A prayer

Father, thank you that I can call you 'Abba,' along with all other Christians. I pray that today there may be a great sense of that universal family, and that women all over the world may commit themselves to rise up to live and work for you.

RG

Genesis 3:1–6 (NJB)

The forbidden fruit

Now, the snake was the most subtle of all the wild animals that Yahweh God had made. It asked the woman, 'Did God really say you were not to eat from any of the trees in the garden?' The woman answered the snake, 'We may eat the fruit of the trees in the garden. But of the fruit of the tree in the middle of the garden God said, "You must not eat it, nor touch it, under pain of death."' Then the snake said to the woman, 'No! You will not die! God knows that the day you eat it your eyes will be opened and you will be like gods, knowing good from evil.' The woman saw that the tree was good to eat and pleasing to the eye, and that it was enticing for the wisdom that it could give. So she took some of its fruit and ate it. She also gave some to her husband who was with her, and he ate it.

This is the age-old story of human temptation; it still analyses how we fall into temptation. The serpent is as yet an attractive and noble-looking creature, more like the fiery serpents of the desert than the worm that crawls on its stomach. The subtlety of the serpent comes out in its overstating the case, so that it allows the woman to correct it—'...only the tree in the middle of the garden!'—also in its flattery, which puts the woman further off her guard: 'You will not die!' Only when her moral guard is well and truly down does she see the attraction of the forbidden fruit.

What is the 'original' sin? It has been suggested that the author was thinking of enticement into Canaanite fertility-rites. More likely it is a presentation of how every departure from our moral principles takes place: proud independence, desire to create our own norms, selective vision. We know perfectly well what we should do, and on the whole we reverence such matters, but this is a special case—just this once! You see, there are special circumstances which override the general rule, etc, etc...

A prayer

Lord God, I know that I blind myself and try to put myself in your place. Give me objectivity and remembrance of your love to hold me back.

HV

continues to keep an open house, although the scale of hospitality in an English episcopal residence is sometimes very much larger.

Beyond that she learnt quickly from attending meetings of the north-west bishops' and wives' group that there was no compulsion to be involved with her husband's work. 'Indeed, a growing number of English wives continue their careers,' she says. 'After a period of assessment and getting to know the diocese I have tried to chase Christian activities that seem appropriate to my gifts and experience.'

But five years after moving to Blackburn, Jennie and the whole family were to have a terrible shock. Jennie was sixty when a routine mammogram led to a diagnosis of breast cancer. Alan and Jennie's only child, David, was doing his GCSEs. The shock experienced by the whole family was immense, but it was faced calmly with prayer. Their belief as a Christian family was that 'all shall be well'.

The breast cancer was dealt with by a biopsy and a course of radiotherapy, but it has left its mark on their lives. 'We now live day by day and do not waste time planning too much for the future,' she explains. But with her usual optimism she brightens up: 'This probably gives us a heightened quality of life and ministry. Once again, crisis became opportunity. Thanks be to God.'

Jennie's prayer

Almighty God and Father,
send your Holy Spirit
to enable us to be aware of your loving presence
   with us this day.

Be in our poverty and our riches,
our sickness and our health,
our successes and our failure,
that, seeking your will in all things,
we may finally come to our eternal home
to be with you for ever.
Through Jesus Christ our Lord,

Amen

Marie Elizabeth Dyer – USA

Fact file

Name: Marie Elizabeth J. Dyer
Date of birth: 22 May 1932
Husband: Mark Dyer, Professor of Theology at Virginia
  Theological Seminary and formerly Bishop of
  Bethlehem, USA
Children: Matthew, 24; John, 21; Jennifer, 19

I feel I have known Marie Elizabeth for a long time, but we have actually met only three times. The first time was at the 1988 Lambeth Conference. David Sheppard, a senior bishop in the Church of England, and his wife Grace invited a small group of other bishops and their wives to join them in a restaurant out in the countryside near Canterbury. The Dyers and the Careys were both invited and so a friendship began.

I did not see Marie Elizabeth again until February 1997 when we were on sabbatical leave in Virginia Seminary and had a meal together, but I have seen Bishop Mark frequently in the intervening years because he represents the Episcopal Church of the United States of America on the Orthodox–Anglican Dialogue. Since George became Archbishop of Canterbury we have travelled to meet many Orthodox Patriarchs, and Mark has often been the American bishop to join the group.

So through him I have followed with interest the career

of Marie Elizabeth, as the first priest to be married to a bishop and with her husband as her boss.

Although I have never met the children, I feel I have followed John and Jennifer through their teenage years and prayed for Matthew, their hydro-encephalic son, during the times he has been seriously ill.

Marie Elizabeth and Mark were our guests at the Old Palace in Canterbury at the end of May 1997 to join in the celebrations marking the arrival of Augustine from Rome, 1400 years ago, to convert the pagan English. It was fun to be together again to share in such a historic occasion, which has shaped our history and given us the living faith we share.

So our paths crossed again, and I am delighted that Marie Elizabeth is sharing her story with us. She is unique to be the first priest spouse of a bishop. Others have joined in that calling now. Her story tells something of the pain and loneliness of being different, but also the joys of her ministry.

Marie Elizabeth Dyer

'I could write a book about being the first woman to be a bishop's wife and a priest,' says Marie Elizabeth. 'This fact was a circumstance of history rather than an earned honour, which brought me joy, pain, amusement and occasionally loneliness among colleagues in my diocese, where I was the boss's wife.'

Marie Elizabeth was born in Johannesburg, South Africa. Her father, from Somerset in England, met and married her mother, who was born in South Africa, when he was the city engineer of Johannesburg. He later became a consulting engineer. Marie Elizabeth had an older brother and a younger sister, and tells us that they were brought up in a loving Christian home. They attended a Presbyterian church where their father was an elder, and when older were encouraged to go to church twice on a Sunday. Marie Elizabeth sang in the choir in the evening service and taught in Sunday School in the morning.

'There was the shadow of the Second World War over my life from seven to thirteen years of age. My father's many brothers and sisters were in England and I had cousins in the service as well as my mother's three brothers, who I knew very well. Even our own minister went to be a chaplain to the troops.' Marie Elizabeth goes on to say, 'I owned my Christianity through the Methodist church because their dynamic minister, also a very holy man, was not sent to war.'

As Marie Elizabeth got older other people's preconceived notions about South Africa burdened her. She says, 'Our cook knew more of my growing pains than my grandmother. As children we were always aware of the fierce inequalities between black and white and also of racial hatred. My father was part of the 'solution' as a great advocate for justice, and as a family we worked on several outreach programmes. The bus strikes and the riots came later, and in those years I was privileged to know and worship with Alan Paton, who was active in fighting for equality and wrote *Cry the Beloved Country*.'

Marie Elizabeth did her BA in South Africa and her teaching diploma in St Andrews, Scotland, and went to Boston in the States to do her MA. Following on from that she achieved a 'first' by being the first woman to graduate from Weson Jesuit School of Theology, made even more remarkable because she was an Episcopalian. Before her ordination in 1978 she taught full time in both elementary and high schools in England, Switzerland, South Africa, the USA and Canada. She has also been a nun, of the

Anglican Order of St Anne, but left before taking her final vows.

Marie Elizabeth met Mark in the late 1960s when they were both attending an annual ecumenical dialogue. She says, 'We can't remember our first conversation. It was probably his response to "Would you like another cup of tea, Father Mark?"' Mark was at that time a Roman Catholic priest. Later they were to meet again when they were in the same class in the University of Ottawa.

'Mark had been a priest for several years before we met,' says Marie Elizabeth, 'and I soon realised that his calling was, to him, one of total commitment to God and to preaching and teaching His word. He was and is one of the few holy men I know.' Mark left the Roman Catholic Church and became an Episcopalian. Their paths crossed again, and they were married in 1971.

Both Mark and Marie Elizabeth had personal crises in their lives before they met. Mark's father died when he was young and Marie Elizabeth's younger sister died when she was only twenty-nine. That made them stronger and more understanding of one another and of other people's lives. It enabled them to cope better when they discovered that their first adopted son had hydro-ancephaly and were told that he would not live beyond his first year. Marie Elizabeth says, 'He has outlived his life expectancy over and over and it has affected our ministry. We have had to deal with the range of feelings a handicapped child engenders, as well as many "theologies" on the will of God.'

Matthew has always lived at home and been cared for by Mark and Marie Elizabeth, with a little outside help when necessary. This means there are many conflicting demands on her time and life is extremely busy. Mark and the children take precedence over her part-time work, which is now as a parish priest, unless there is a crisis in the church and then the family are always understanding and helpful.

Marie Elizabeth Dyer – USA

Marie Elizabeth was ordained in the diocese of Massachusetts when Mark was still a priest and she says, 'He has always helped and encouraged me in my ministry. However, when he became a bishop it required me to leave my part-time work in the children's hospital in Boston where I was deeply fulfilled and challenged as a chaplain. But his ministry has always been an integral part of my life, both as a priest and a bishop's wife, so I moved to Bethlehem where I have since been a part-time priest.'

There have been many challenges in Bethlehem for Marie Elizabeth. Shortly after they arrived there was a major school teachers' strike and she and Mark found themselves involved in establishing an alternative programme to keep the children safe and occupied, to enable the parents to continue working. Bethlehem is famous for its steel industry, but downsizing over the years has been an ongoing concern and they have found themselves helping the wealthy unemployed to come to terms with little prospect of future employment. Marie Elizabeth calls it 'my ministry of presence among these people to give them a sense of hope and self-worth'.

Prayer is very important to Marie Elizabeth. It is from this she gets her spiritual strength, while the rhythm of the services in her own church and the services she attends with Mark are opportunities to share and grow. She has a spiritual director who recognises her priesthood and is both challenging and compassionate.

'I think and pray any place and any time,' says Marie Elizabeth.

Marie Elizabeth's prayer

Dear Lord, our Heavenly Father,

33

Help us to be your servants to those:
> HUNGRY for peace, not division; people whose souls clamour for the sustenance of justice, an end to crimes of violence and greed; to those longing for a night's sleep without gnawing hunger, the fear of starvation.

Empower us to feed your sheep, your lambs.

Help us to be your servants to those:
> THIRSTY for water, unpolluted water, parched for understanding, for living water.

Enable us to quench their thirst, to offer them the Blood of Christ.

Help us to be your servants to those:
> STRANGERS who live next door, the handicapped, the addicted, all outcasts.
> Remind us they are your friends, made in your image.

Help us to be your servants to those:
> NAKED in their loss by fire, water or tornado; exposed by the media; unable to hide their emotions.

Give us grace to clothe their needs.

Help us to be your servants to those:
> SICK grown-ups and children, waiting for diagnoses, transplants or cures; people sick from the world's ills and disappointments.

Beloved Physician, heal them, we pray.

Help us to be your servants to those:
> IMPRISONED, awaiting sentence or parole; imprisoned by debt, or an abusive relationship, locked in prisons that have no bars.

Help us to free them, to speak of your love.

Forgive us our failures. May we see you in others each day of our lives.

This we pray, for Christ's sake,

Amen

Sussanna Ebo and
Esther Olajide – Nigeria

Fact file

Name: Sussanna Ada Ebo
Date of birth: 4 April 1933
Husband: Samuel Chukuma Ebo, Bishop of the diocese
  of Orlu, Nigeria
Children: Ngozi Grace Abara, married with three
  children; Chinedu Uche Ebo, married with two children
First language: Igbo

Fact file

Name: Esther Modupe Olajide
Date of birth: 28 December 1936
Husband: Gideon I. Ola Olajide, Bishop of Ibadan,
  Nigeria
First language: Yoruba

Nigeria is a country that we have not yet visited. Two visits
have been arranged, but both were cancelled. The first time
was because elections were called when we were due to be
there and the church cancelled the visit because they said they
could not guarantee our safety. A year later, when the dates

were in the diary again, there was a mini coup and our safety could not be guaranteed so the visit was once again cancelled.

Nigeria is the largest and fastest growing province in the Anglican communion. There are sixty dioceses and these are now split into three provinces. The Archbishop of Nigeria is in overall charge and in particular charge of Province One. He has appointed two bishops to care for the other two provinces. The inauguration of the three provinces and the presentation of their archbishops was in October 1997.

It is an exciting challenge to the Church because the upsurge of Islam, particularly in the north, is spreading and the building of mosques, often beside churches, is not unusual. But the Anglican Church is the largest single denomination as well as the fastest growing.

Nigeria has recently celebrated the 150th anniversary of Anglican Christianity in the country. It has grown from a small mission venture of faith by the Church Missionary Society, always kept securely grounded in its biblical foundation and commitment to that evangelical stance.

Orlu Diocese, where Sussanna's husband is the first bishop, was carved out of Owerri Diocese in 1984 and has since been divided into three further dioceses because of the rapid growth of Christianity. It is a largely rural diocese with a deep commitment to rural mission.

Sussanna is very active alongside her husband and I am delighted that she has shared her story with us. What is most impressive about her contribution is the way the Bible guides her every action. She is grounded in Scripture and lives it out daily in her home and in all her dealings with people. Is this something that we in the West have lost?

In contrast to Orlu Diocese, Ibadan is largely urban and the largest city in West Africa. The Church is growing rapidly, with an emphasis on student ministry, Bible study and fellowship ministry and church planting in the diocese, and Esther takes a full part in it all alongside her husband.

She shares her story with us in a delightful and often humorous way.

Women in Nigeria form the lifeline of the Church and the vanguard of evangelism, mission and ministry. This was summed up very aptly way back in the early 1900s by Bishop Shanakan, when he wrote:

Oh! brave women of Emeke [a town near Owerri]
May you long have the power of your fine arms;
And may you die with the light of God's Grace in
  your souls!
How much the fathers owe to you cannot possibly
  be estimated.

Sussanna Ebo

Sussanna has always had a strong sense of duty as a clergyman's wife. To a great extent her cheerful absorption of responsibilities came from a very active Christian upbringing. She says, 'My experience of the Christian faith in the early years channelled my mode of life and has helped me greatly in knowing the word of God and witnessing for God.'

Both her parents were active members of the Church. Her father, a timber trader who died at the age of eighty, was pastor's warden and a committee member of the church. Her mother, still living at the age of eighty-four, contributed immensely in the promotion of women's work in the Church. She now lives with Sussanna and Samuel.

As a child Sussanna remembers enjoying painting and the children's services and Sunday School classes. She grew into a devout teenager and sang in the choir. She still loves singing.

She met Samuel in 1958 when he led a group of youth leaders from Trinity College, Umuahia, for a workshop at her youth group. She was a member of the group and a primary school teacher. Sussanna and Samuel were married in the same year.

She doesn't recall being 'scared' of his calling to the priesthood, saying that this was 'because my upbringing was properly rooted in knowing my God and I was brought up in the fear of God. I was trained in the mission school as a teacher, and thereby well equipped for my calling and able to fulfil all the functions to give the right type of leadership to the church women.'

Nevertheless, Sussanna strives for hard targets in her calling as a clergy wife. First priorities are the family and helping her husband. She also believes that she is called to make her home a kind of demonstration parish and to welcome strangers and visitors at any time. This means that on a daily basis she faces dozens of conflicting demands upon her time. 'People with health, family, church, personal and societal problems often visit at a very wrong time of day without any consideration and would like you to attend to them at all costs,' she says. 'On the other hand, I appreciate God's guidance and protection with this enormous task.'

She has a clear-cut definition of her role as the wife of a bishop:

First, she says, she aims: 'To do good to my husband and not to harm him, all the days of my life. I will be a blessing to him and not a curse'.

Second, she aims: 'To be temperate, dedicated and have seriousness of character. That is, being thoughtful, earnest, sober, sedate, responsible, not frivolous or reckless or given to trifling'.

Third, she aims: 'To be a good example of self-control. To keep my body in temperance, soberness and chastity'.

Finally, her aim is 'to be faithful in all things and in dispensing whatever is entrusted to my care'.

As the old axiom goes, 'cleanliness is next to godliness'. Sussanna is a determined believer in keeping her home as a model for parishioners. This means making a priority of housework and laundry. Her objectives are: 'To take care of myself including what I wear. My clothes may not be expensive, but they should be clean and decent. To see that the members of the family eat regularly, including myself. I also try to force my husband to take something before he leaves home in the morning, and if he is away I try to get him a snack box and a flask for something to drink,' she adds.

Sussanna is equally clear about what she has learnt since becoming a bishop's wife. She believes that to be serious in all her undertakings is extremely important. In this way she is intent on being faithful to the fruits of the Spirit. 'I have learnt to be faithful in dispensing whatever is entrusted to my care. I have learnt to keep my head above water, particularly at this time when the get-rich-quick mania grips almost everybody.' She quotes two verses from Proverbs: 'Better is a little with the fear of the Lord than great treasure and trouble with it' (15:16), and 'He who is greedy for unjust gain makes trouble for his household, but he who hates bribes will live' (15:27).

Her rejection of materialism based on her biblical faith finds its outworking in social ministry. This ministry, like her home life, is well organised. Her priority is evangelism, but from that flows a leadership training workshop, Bible study groups, a prayer and healing workshop. In fact the list seems endless: she also helps with young people's work and the adult education workshop and is involved with an action and outreach unit. With the unit, for example, she visits prisoners 'to nourish their body and soul', and schools and isolated church prayer groups.

Nigeria has seen startling church growth in recent years. Nevertheless, she is frank about some of the problems facing the diocese. She lists these as 'leadership tussles, scrambling for power, lack of spiritual maturity and inability to speak out'. On the other hand, she describes the opportunities open to the people of the diocese in terms of the love and blessing of God. 'There are a lot of committed Christians who sacrifice their time and talents in the developments in the diocese. The clergy and laity work together with love and understanding in the appointment of posts in the Church.

'The problems do not affect my life and thinking because God pilots the affairs of the diocese and He is in control. The opportunities give me joy and happiness and increase my faith and trust in God with prayers. Prayer changes things,' she declares.

Sussanna's prayer

O Holy Spirit, Giver of light and life,
Impart to us thoughts higher than our own thoughts, and prayers better than our own prayers, and powers beyond our powers, that we may spend and be spent in the ways of love and goodness, after the perfect image of our Lord and Saviour, Jesus Christ.

Let us praise and thank the Lord, who has been our refuge and strength and ever-present help in trouble. God continues to reign as all wise and as almighty. Rejoice, for God is here among us. He continues to be our sure refuge and strength in the coming years.

Amen

Esther Olajide

The decision of Esther's family to convert to Christianity resulted in intolerable suffering and the persecution of her parents. They were born into a traditional, polygamous culture; Christianity only came to Nigeria in 1842. 'My father showed to all his children the scars from a knife stab on his left side and whip lash on his back to make us realise what he had gone through,' she remembers.

Esther's mother came from the royal family of the region. She married into a big polygamous family, all living happily together under the same roof. 'She was a good disciplinarian but kind, motherly and liberal. She was loved by all as she cared for those around her. The palace and the community offered her several traditional chieftancies, but she opted for the Christian one in order to hold to her faith and avoid fetish activities.' She held the post of 'Iya Ijo' (the lay Christian woman leader) at St Michael's Anglican Church, Ilara-Mokin, from 1953 until she died in 1977.

Esther was one of eight children, but three of her siblings died in infancy. 'My teenage years were rough and tough because the first daughter traditionally has to be groomed in such a way as to be able to play the role of mother to other children in later years. So that made my mother harsher on me than the others.' Such grooming for responsibility was spotted by her teachers at primary school, who in spite of her age made the young girl the school prefect a full year early. Her leadership role has continued in all of her schools and in her work up till today.

She remembers going to church services carrying a Bible and hymn book and following her parents on evangelistic outreach. At Sunday School the catechism was taught, with stories from the Bible and hymns. The children memorised the Ten Commandments, the collects and verses in the Bible in their local languages.

'I attended church school, where worship was held in the morning, before and after break and before we closed for the day. The first lesson from Monday to Friday was Bible Knowledge. Moral Instruction was taught two to three times a week,' she recalls clearly.

One great disappointment in Esther's life was her lack of a secondary education. She failed in three attempts. First, she was rejected by a Roman Catholic school because she would not convert; at another school she had to withdraw due to financial problems, and on the third occasion a scholarship that was meant for her was passed on to the daughter of the district clergy superintendent. She became a pupil-teacher and then saved up for teacher training.

Esther trained to be a teacher through a great deal of hardship. She had to struggle to pay her way through education by herself. Her father was a subsistence farmer and tailor with several wives and children and was fully occupied with providing for an extended family. It was her mother's encouragement and influence which helped Esther achieve her goals. She was able to do petty jobs after school hours and during holidays to earn some money to pay her fees and buy books. When she later trained as a student nurse in England, she sent money from the pittance she earned to help support her younger brother in secondary school.

It was in the long vacation that she met Gideon, who knew members of her family. He and his classmate and friend, the present Archbishop of Nigeria, the Most Rev. Adetiloye, belonged to the first generation of very young priests, having entered seminary at twenty-one to train as catechists. The college authorities, she says, 'for reasons best known to themselves changed the course', and they became priests. Their progress was watched throughout the Christian community with great interest.

'Personally, I was delighted that they gave good account of themselves both academically and spiritually,' says Esther. 'On their tasks as young priests they performed well and justified the confidence reposed in them.' Gideon threw himself into his work as pastor, teacher and youth worker for the diocese. Esther visited him in his two stations, one in the city, the other in the countryside.

Marriage to a clergyman has affected Esther's life in many different ways. 'It was a total surrender of self to the companionship that marriage demanded. Our local adage says, "When the snail moves, its shell moves with it." When I consented to marry him and I joined him in England, I gave up the teaching profession for which I had trained and took to nursing. In God's providence He used the two professions to prepare me for the future which we have to share together.'

Their life together has been one of constant moves. The first was to London, to a theological college; later Gideon was a lecturer at Immanuel College in Nigeria and then Warden of five university halls of residence. During this period Esther was variously college nurse and nursing sister as well as participating fully in his ministry.

In 1979 Gideon became provost of the cathedral in Ibadan. As well as assuming the task of being provost's wife and assistant to the bishop's wife, Esther headed the satellite clinic of the Ife University Health Centre in the town as principal nursing sister. Only three years later they were on the move again to Ilesha, and she was bishop's wife and leader of the Interdenominational Women's Association. During this period she gave up her work as a nurse because the work in the diocese was too demanding.

'Seven years, seven months and seven days later we were on the move again to Ibadan, the biggest diocese in western

Sussanna Ebo and Esther Olajide – Nigeria

Nigeria, the mother of five dioceses, two of which have been created since we came to Ibadan. What is left is still looking forward to being subdivided into two or more dioceses.'

Together, Esther says, they have had to give leadership to interdenominational and inter-religious organisations, and relate to government and build up organisations for the welfare of the community. 'These call for continuous and continual prayer and total reliance on the strength and wisdom which the Lord alone supplies,' she says.

One of the greatest struggles of their life together has been their inability to have children, a source of great distress to couples the world over. But in Nigeria the expectations are particularly high. 'In our society people begin to ask questions about the expectation of a child weeks after a marriage. It is a society which will urge the husband to take another wife if a child is not forthcoming in the first three to five years of marriage. A wife can be denied her legitimate rights in several ways, by being made to run from pillar to post and spending all her livelihood to achieve her heart's desire.'

It was a frustrating and harrowing experience, she remembers, for the wife of a leading churchman. At times, when questions were thrown at her, it could be demeaning and degrading. 'To take an unpopular stand in such a case and to be sure that it is a Christian stand and to be ready to bear the insult and reproach and at the same time to hope against hope in a society like ours, can only be done by the grace of God alone,' she declares. 'That one does not collapse under the stress or yield to the suggestions lovingly made by people out of good intentions, but which may give one a happiness at the loss of a holiness, is only by the strength the Lord supplies.'

They did not have to adopt children: her sister-in-law died, leaving four children, and this tragedy was compounded by another when her younger brother died, leaving five

45

children. This affected Esther badly and the shock made her ill. She had almost starved to see him through primary, secondary and university education, followed by marriage, and then he died at the age of thirty-nine. 'There are others in the extended family and in the church family who relate to us not less than one's own biological children, and we thank God for them,' Esther reflects.

When Esther made the decision to become a full-time bishop's wife this was because she knew she would be needed to travel with Gideon around the diocese. Nevertheless it was tough, because she was just a month away from promotion to a higher grade. She remembers it looking a 'ridiculous' choice to her colleagues, but after prayer she knew what to do.

'Callers and visitors of all categories stream in from dawn to dusk, and by nature and conviction we do not want to turn anyone away. It is nerve-racking coping with this and domestic chores and administrative demands and one is hardly given time to eat.' She remarks wryly that management techniques on prioritising time just do not fit in to the African culture. She describes sleep as the only antidote.

Her account of the role of a bishop's wife is clear, detailed and filled with humour: 'I am the unpaid assistant to the bishop and the diocese, his constant companion in most of his travels. I am his chief cook, as he prefers to eat some particular foods which he cherishes only when prepared by his wife, not minding whether I am as tired or more tired than himself when we are back home. Add to this, hospitality to statutory diocesan committees. I am expected and have to be the mother to all in the diocese and to lead all the women's organisations both ecclesiastical and secular. I continue by my life and lips to teach the young ones of the family and the church as they look to me for guidance and counsel. Like my husband, I represent the diocese to the world and the secular world receives me as Mama Bishop.'

Esther's prayer

We thank you, our Father and our God, for your gracious dealings with us.

We pray that in our work and witness you will enable us by your Holy Spirit, that we may always do the things that please you. Daily uphold us, Lord, that we may uplift your name, through Jesus Christ our Lord,

Amen

Chitra Fernando – Sri Lanka

Fact file

Name: Chitra Fernando
Date of birth: 25 August 1933
Husband: Kenneth Fernando, Bishop of Colombo,
  Sri Lanka
Children: Three sons: Premendra, 33, married to
  Priyanka with a daughter, Prasadhini; Shanthikumar,
  30, married to Lakshii; Kumarasiri, (adopted) 25,
  married to Surethra

Kenneth Fernando was consecrated Bishop of Colombo, the capital of Sri Lanka, in December 1992. We were privileged to be there, and my husband consecrated him. I met Chitra for the first time on that occasion.

This island in the Indian Ocean, off the southern coast of India, was known as Ceylon until it became independent from the British in 1972 and was renamed the Republic of Sri Lanka. When I was a child, tea from Ceylon was considered to be the very best for a really good 'cuppa'. Sri Lanka's tropical location ensures perennially high temperatures. When we were there in December it was extremely hot and humid.

The population of the country is made up of three ethnic groups – Sinhalese, Tamil and Muslim. The majority of the Sinhalese are Buddhists, while the Tamils are overwhelmingly Hindu. Only about 7 per cent of the population are Christian.

The service of consecration was held in the cathedral, set in the church compound with the diocesan offices and the bishop's house. I remember it as a very long service but full of colour, symbolism and cultural liturgical elements. I was very moved by the symbolic 'washing of feet' by Kenneth of three people representing the flock that he was being commissioned to care for. Various badges of office of a bishop were presented to him by representatives of the congregation.

My thoughts at the time were of how fortunate these people were to have Kenneth and Chitra to care for them. Both are extremely gifted and give themselves unstintingly to care for the people in this very troubled island, torn apart by political unrest and ethnic conflict.

While in the country we were able to see some of the many projects that the Church has set up to help the very poor and needy in their society. We also travelled up country into the diocese of Kurunagala, which is very rural, and saw some of the fine work being done by the Church there.

I am very pleased that Chitra agreed to contribute her story, as I know the situation within the country will then be better understood and more prayed for. It is a country that does not often become international news, but it is another place in the Anglican communion that is hurting.

Chitra Fernando

At the time of writing, Anglicans in the diocese of Colombo are most distressed about the hostile ethnic conflict between Sinhalese and Tamils. The Anglican Church has the unique advantage of being composed of 50 per cent from each rival group. This factor, says Chitra Fernando, the wife of the Bishop of Colombo, 'gives Anglicans more than any other Christian denomination in Sri Lanka the opportunity to present to our people a pattern of harmonious living which supersedes ethnic differences. Unfortunately,' she concedes ruefully, 'Anglicans have not always in the past used this opportunity to maximum advantage.' But she points to the sterling work of Anglican clergy in the north of the country, who are looking after congregations to the best of their ability under such hostile circumstances. In spite of the war situation, Chitra and her husband Kenneth have visited Jaffna, at the centre of the conflict, as often as they can.

Kenneth has been in the forefront of peacemaking efforts, even to the extent of meeting the elusive leader of the LTTE – one of the groupings – and actively participating in the negotiations for peace. The tense atmosphere that prevails in the country is such that anyone who works for peaceful negotiation rouses suspicion and hostility.

'So it goes without saying that our lives are at risk. Our home in Piliyandala was raided by the police, on false information supplied by our enemies that it was an LTTE arsenal. My husband has often been castigated by the newspapers as a supporter of the LTTE. However, he continues to assert that peace is the only option for us Christians and to confer with individuals and organisations which are committed to the peace process,' she declares.

Although Chitra has always had a passion for justice, it is as a bishop's wife that she has been able to witness the potential of the Church for bringing about peace and harmony. Her travels with Kenneth have brought home at first hand the trials and difficulties of clergy and their families who serve in the war-torn areas, and she herself has attended various meetings and conferences on the current national crisis. 'Our home has often been the centre of such discussion, to which persons of other ethnic groups and religious persuasions have been invited. Consequently I have realised more than ever before the significant role that Christians can play in promoting national harmony,' she says.

Chitra was born in a town called Moratuwa, thirteen miles south of Colombo. Her mother was a teacher and her father was a businessman. 'My parents' legacy', she says, to all four sisters and one brother, 'was a sound education.'

'We were never rich but our parents provided us with all our basic needs, sacrificing their own leisure in order to ensure a happy home life. I consider myself singularly fortunate to have been nurtured in the Christian faith at home and in school as well as in church and Sunday School, but chiefly at home.'

She points out that neither of her parents were overtly religious, but that they both had a 'deep and firm faith in God'. This faith became particularly apparent to the children in times of crisis and economic hardship.

'I was six years old when the Second World War began. Our school buildings were commandeered by the British Army. But our school continued to function in three large houses situated at fairly convenient distances from one another. I do not think that my education was affected in any way by the war situation. In fact we learnt to do with very little material comforts and get our priorities in the right order.'

She is particularly grateful for the sound religious education she received from her teachers in both the day school and the Sunday School. She attended an English-speaking school, but recalls that her fluency in her own language, Sinhalese, came from Sunday School classes which were conducted in this language. It was a fifteen-year Sunday School course, very different from the ad hoc programmes of

Sunday teaching offered to children in most other countries. When she had completed this course she became a Sunday School teacher.

Chitra and Kenneth met at the University of Sri Lanka, where she studied English, history and economics and later completed a course for a diploma in education, specialising in teaching English as a second language. They were both members of the Student Christian Movement, where many enduring friendships came about as a result of the early morning prayer cells on Wednesday, weekly Bible study sessions, regular choir practices and worship on Sundays.

'Kenneth and I were good friends for a long time before we decided to get married. When I look back on those early years, I realise that from the beginning I regarded him as a person I could trust, absolutely.'

She knew from the start that Kenneth was planning to be ordained after he had completed his first degree in classics and then his further theological studies. 'Before I had ever begun to think of him as my future husband I had seen his contributions to various magazines and the inputs he made at our Bible studies, seminars and conferences. Above all I greatly admired his sincerity of purpose, since I knew that, though he could have chosen any other profession if he so wished, his decision to become a priest of God was irrevocable.'

Their courtship was to be interrupted when Chitra began her teaching career in 1955 and Kenneth went to study theology at Cuddesdon Theological College in Oxford. She recalls that they kept very close contact through letters for those four years and found, in comparing notes, that they had often even bought the same books. Chitra's interest in theology, stimulated by her relationship with Kenneth, was to chart a similar course. 'We've always been on the same wavelength with regard to attitudes and values and in living out the Christian faith,' she says. Although

Chitra's theological enquiry was never for the purpose of sitting an examination, she has kept reading deeply over many years.

In January 1960 they began their married life together in a slum parish, St John's, Mattakkuliya, where Kenneth was assistant curate for the next two years. She recalls: 'Our home, the church and the small garden surrounding it formed a veritable oasis for all the poor children in the area. I taught some of them at St John's School, which was only a little distance away from our home. It was a co-educational school with Sinhala and Tamil streams so we were able to form links with the wider community through the children, Buddhists, Hindus and Muslims as well as Christians.'

She remembers how the young people of the parish were galvanised into action and a first-aid centre for the poor and several other social service activities began. In addition to these parish activities, Chitra was working with her enthusiastic principal at school to raise the standard of education. It was a poorly equipped school, but eventually their efforts resulted in the school being upgraded in 1962. These first two years were to set a pattern for the years ahead.

Wherever Kenneth moved, Chitra kept an even balance between her teaching career and the parish. She was helped by the fact that he took as much interest in her activities at school as she did in the parish.

'We had decided at the very outset that I should play a supportive role in my husband's parish ministry, and not that of a second curate!' But this partnership in parenting and ministry, in which they both clearly defined each other's roles and supported each other, worked well for them both. After nearly thirty years of teaching, Chitra eventually became Director-Secretary of the National Council of Churches Department of Education in 1981. Two years later Kenneth was to become Director of the Ecumenical Institute for Study and Dialogue. 'Until I had built up my own team of resource persons my husband was my chief resource person. He gladly put not only his time and expertise, but his chauffeuring services as well, at our disposal, because he, more than any other person I know, recognises the importance of the task of Christian education.

'Our husband and wife partnership in education began nearly twenty years ago,' she says proudly, 'when we produced a textbook on Christianity for O level students.' Even after Kenneth was consecrated bishop of the diocese of Colombo they continued to work together in the production of course material for both day and Sunday School teachers of Christianity.

'I had never wanted to be anything else but a teacher in high school,' she says frankly. 'Nor have I ever desired to live in any other country. I was not even greatly attracted by foreign travel.' However, foreign travel was to find her. In 1975 she was chosen as a delegate to the World Council of Churches Assembly in Nairobi. She remembers being exposed there to exciting new trends in education. During the Assembly she became involved in a study section entitled Education for Liberation and Community. This, she said, enabled her to widen horizons and think deeply about an education which can liberate people to live in community.

Chitra's valiant work for Christian education has not been easy. Although religion is a compulsory subject in Sri Lanka, the lack of Christian teachers has been a great frustration. Most Christian students, therefore, are forced to learn Buddhism or Hinduism instead of Christianity. In 1985 Chitra inaugurated a voluntary teacher service, which now includes over a hundred teachers who give lessons in Christianity on behalf of the Church. 'But we have to work hard to make this teacher service financially viable,' she sighs.

'I have also been keenly interested in women's issues,'

she says. 'Until recently I was an active member of a secular organisation, Voice of Women, which still continues to play a significant role in highlighting the problems women face. I am also a member of the Mothers' Union and of the Diocesan Board of Women's Work, which undertakes a number of social service projects among women.'

It was the visit of a Canadian woman priest, the Rev. Dr June Maffin, in February 1994 which inspired Chitra and a small group of women to establish the Support Network for the Ordination of Women (with the appropriate acronym SNOW). This group includes men as well as women in its membership.

Chitra openly says that she is not comfortable being defined as a bishop's wife, because she does not consider this to be her primary calling. 'I continue to play the role of a priest's wife, in that our home is open to people at all times and I share in the pastoral care extended to them by my husband. Now, more than ever before, I join my husband in the social activities of all our churches, even those of other denominations. Within the first two years of his episcopate I visited every church in the diocese, including the churches in the war-torn areas.'

But now, she says, she has to be more selective in travelling with Kenneth, who often spends seven to ten days at a time in different areas of his far-flung diocese. She chooses carefully, going with him to areas where she can also conduct business of her own, such as an education conference, while he is there.

'In our daily life I have resisted the pressure to conform to the social expectations of people regarding a bishop and a bishop's wife. We still maintain a spartan lifestyle. We often have people staying with us, but our guests soon become part of the family and share in everything we do. We do not go in for formal entertaining, especially in view of the poverty in our country and the ethnic conflict, but we try to invite a clergy family for dinner once a week so that we can get to know the children and give them an opportunity to communicate their special interests.'

The major problem Chitra faces is finding the right balance between her work, her supportive role to Kenneth and time for the family. They are singularly fortunate that their sons and wives live with them at Bishop's House, in the Sri Lankan tradition of the extended family. She explains: 'If they lived away from us we would hardly have been able to visit them. One of my greatest joys is talking and singing to my little granddaughter, Prasadhini, for short spells in between my varied activities.'

The household has no servants, so each member of the family shares the housework. Kenneth and Chitra begin the day with a walk at the unearthly hour of five in the morning, followed by exercises. She describes this precious time as an opportunity to 'iron out problems, share jokes and talk'. The whole family are early risers and join them at 5.30 in the kitchen, where 'the conversation rolls on'. They come together as a family again in the evening, when they combine dinner with watching the television or simply catching up with each other.

Chitra has found that such good organisation is vital in getting priorities balanced. She has a similarly practical attitude to her spirituality, which is based on the firm conviction that work and worship are one and the same thing. She is always at her office for a time of quiet and meditation a good hour before anyone else arrives. Meditative Bible reading challenges her to adopt new ways of doing things and, she says, can even change the focus of her work.

Chitra Fernando – Sri Lanka

Chitra's prayer

O Lord our God,

We thank you for placing us in a country which is full of opportunities to serve you.

We thank you for the multi-ethnic, multi-religious and multi-cultural character of our people, which challenges us to seek unity in diversity.

Help the Church in our land to be one in their witness to Christ's activity in our land towards peace and reconciliation. Enable all Christians to play their part in bringing all communities together as a rainbow people, enriching one another with their diverse gifts, languages and cultures.

Lead us into the unknown future, keep us faithful to yourself until your Kingdom comes into its own in our midst.

Amen

Barbara George – Australia

Fact file

Name: Barbara George
Date of birth: 5 July 1941
Husband: Ian Gordon Combe George, Archbishop of
  Adelaide, province of South Australia
Children: Sarah, born 1966, married to Gregor Brown
  with one child; Samuel, born 1968, died 1990

George and I first met Barbara and Ian in January 1991
in Canberra, where Ian was the assistant bishop. We were
there for the World Council of Churches when George
was Archbishop of Canterbury designate. We enjoyed
their company enormously but were aware of the deep
pain within them both so soon after the death of their son.
Barbara shares something of that with us in her story. They
have since moved to Adelaide.

Ian and Barbara came to Lambeth Palace for a meal
with us in January 1997, when they were over in England
on study leave. It was a good opportunity to plan further
the official visit George and I were making to their diocese
in July of that year. We have since had a wonderful
time in Adelaide, staying in their home for three nights.
The programme was interesting and varied, allowing us
a chance to glimpse into many areas of life that the Church
is involved in. It is very active in its welfare programmes

for all ages and is doing a wonderful work among the homeless.

It is always a privilege for us to be with our colleagues in different parts of the Anglican Communion and to broaden our knowledge of the rich, vibrant work going on for the sake of the gospel.

Barbara has shared her very moving and interesting story with us, and I know she has not found it easy. In fact, she acknowledges that she is one of over fifty bishops' wives in Australia, who all have their different stories, full of interest and inspiration, and she wishes that their insights could have been included.

Barbara George

Although Barbara is delighted to share her story in this book, she wants to point out that it comes from the perspective of someone who has been privileged never to face persecution because of race or religion, who has never feared for her life in the face of such persecution, and who has never been forced to go hungry. Barbara continues, 'For this I give thanks. Compared to those who have proclaimed their faith in such circumstances, my story is a pale shadow. For them, some of the things which have troubled me may seem trivial and hard to understand. I hope that sharing our stories will help us to accept each other as we are.'

Has the Church thought through how to deal with women's ministry? Barbara George thinks that the Church is yet to fully come to terms with the transition from celibate to married clergy. But her response to her husband's ministry was to choose her own direction in her family and career while remaining solidly supportive. She admits that her pattern of life might have been much the same had she married a lawyer, doctor or engineer, but adds, 'I think it was made more difficult by the Church's expectation that vocation should place the demands of a priest's calling above all else, including spouse and children, and then making very few concessions to the problems this situation generates. It is pleasing that young clergy couples seem to be more aware of these problems and are able to develop strategies for coping right from the start.

'Now I can hear all those traditional voices saying that the solution to my situation would have been to throw myself into my husband's ministry, to participate more and find my fulfilment that way. But I don't think that many women these days would accept this as the only solution, and I would hazard a guess that most women with similar backgrounds to mine who had the sense of vocation that this requires would be more inclined to offer themselves for ordination or a related career than to play the traditional support role,' says Barbara.

The ordination of women, she believes, has provided opportunities to rethink the impact of ministry on clergy marriages. 'I welcome the new perspectives this is providing. The three-hundred-year-old transition phase from celibate to married clergy has gone on long enough. I hope it does not take as long for the Church to adjust to the new patterns of ministry that have been emerging in recent years.'

Although she has lived in Australia for over thirty years, Barbara's story begins in the United States, in Westchester County, just north of New York City. 'Like all Americans I trace my origins to outside America, and like most I am a mixture of nationalities. Mother's family were descendants of the English Puritans and Dad's family were from Sweden. His father, a printer, arrived in New York at the end of the nineteenth century with some new printing machinery for the *New York Times*. He decided to stay and sent for his young bride from Sweden.'

This family pattern was repeated, Barbara says, when at the age of twenty-four she emigrated to Australia with her Australian husband. 'But those first twenty-four years were spent in the United States in and around New York City, and I had no inkling of what was in store for me.'

Barbara has one older brother, but because he went to boarding school she grew up as if she were an only child. She remembers being happy and having a fairly uneventful childhood. The family moved several times because her father was a consulting engineer. Each time, she says, it was difficult to make a new life with new friends and new activities. But she was a good student and this gave her a focus.

'Neither of my parents were Anglican and my becoming an Anglican (or Episcopalian) was due to the proximity of the local Episcopal church, not because of any religious conviction. My father's background was Lutheran, but he was never involved with the church. Mother had a strong faith but was not wedded to any particular denomination.'

In fact, the church did not play any large part in Barbara's early years. Although she attended church, she was never part of a Sunday School, and had no serious Christian instruction until she was confirmed. Nevertheless, she recalls that the confirmation classes must have whetted her interest, because when she first went to college she chose some courses in religious studies, although she did not pursue this interest further until much later in life. 'Needless to say, when some years later I became engaged to an Anglican theological student, I was totally in the dark about what my life as the wife of a priest would be,' she admits.

She met Ian in New York City. Her first foray into university education at Vassar College had not set the world on fire. This is a prestigious institution, one of the so-called Ivy League colleges, but despite the achievement of getting there Barbara decided that it wasn't for her after completing a year and a half of the course. 'I was not happy there and was not doing well in my studies. Much to everyone's distress I left and went to live and work in New York City. This set the stage for meeting my husband-to-be,' she says.

Shortly afterwards, a Vassar friend asked Barbara to go to a Christmas party with 'some one a friend of hers had met'! The afternoon was New York winter weather at its worst, cold with sleet and slush. The Christmas lights were bright and the city was buzzing with people rushing here and there amid all the sights and sounds of Christmas. Barbara continues, 'But I was cold, my feet were wet and I was late. I dashed into my friend's apartment to change before going out and found that my date, about whom I knew absolutely nothing, was already there. My feet and ankles were muddy, my hair drooped in dripping strands which stuck to my face. All I wanted to do was flee. Inwardly I cringed at the thought of what a sight I must have been. Standing there looking at me with a bemused expression was a tall, pleasant-looking man with thinning brown hair, kind eyes and a wonderful smile. My spirits lifted slightly.'

They were soon to sink again when he was introduced as an Australian theological student at General Seminary. 'Oh dear, I really did not know what to expect. I had never met a theological student before and the stereotypical images – boring, holy and all that – raced through my mind. It was not an auspicious beginning, but we found that we enjoyed each other's company and ended up talking late into the night. Among other things, I learnt a great deal about Australia.'

When Barbara returned to her parents for Christmas, she happened to mention the fact that she had met a very interesting Australian. Conversation stopped and focused on her. 'Later that night, my mother sat on my bed and said, "You wouldn't go to live in Australia, would you?"

I hooted my derision: "I've only just met the man!" but Mother saw the signs, and it was not long afterwards that Ian George and I decided to be married.'

It was either optimism or a spirit of adventure, Barbara says. She adds that others might point to faith which made her willing to embark on marriage to a priest in a strange new country. 'I would just put it down to the fact that love is blind. I had absolutely no idea what I was getting myself into. My husband and I have been working out the consequences ever since, both good and bad.'

Ian had trained and practised as a lawyer in Adelaide, South Australia, before realising that he had a vocation to the priesthood. It was unusual at that time for an Australian to be trained in America. Barbara remembers that the great majority of Australians looked to the English as mentors in many aspects of life. 'When Ian and I met on that cold winter night in 1962 he was about halfway through his three-year course. I had not experienced the long process of decision-making that had preceded his offering himself for ordination, and I had very little understanding of the ramifications and responsibilities associated with that decision. Coming from the background I did, my expectations of a clerical marriage were vastly different from his, although at that time I don't think either of us realised it.'

Before taking the big step of returning to Australia with his new bride, Ian was given an assistant curacy in a parish just outside New York. This decision was wisely made to give him some experience of the American Church and to give Barbara some time to adjust to married life before taking off for Australia. 'I very soon became all too acutely aware of my lack of experience of church life. I think the biggest shock was the fact that Ian's commitment to his vocation was the primary focus of his life. To be fair, he had tried to make this clear to me before we were married but it did not really make an impact until we were in the hurly burly of parish life.

'I think I really expected that priesthood was going to be like any other occupation. As well as the growing realisation that my husband was married to the Church first and me second, there was the shock of encountering a whole world of ecclesiastical etiquette and culture of which I had been totally unaware. All these things were very unsettling but were pushed aside in anticipation of our trip to Australia.'

Barbara took a job to earn money for the journey, which ensured that she was not too involved in parish life at this time. 'In retrospect, I see a whole range of activities which continued to be my "other" as the Church was my husband's "other". First it was becoming adjusted in a new country and a new culture, then children came along. Like all other young clergy families we had a number of moves in our early life. Probably the most unusual one was when we were sent to the outback for a few years, to the rocket-testing range, Woomera, in the mid-north of South Australia.

'Woomera was like a transplanted suburb in the middle of nowhere, a square mile of town with about five thousand residents. Among the things happening there were attempts by the European Launcher Development Organisation, a consortium of English, French, Italian and German interests, to put a satellite in orbit; they never succeeded, but some of the failures were quite spectacular,' she remembers.

Before their two children were at school, Barbara had completed a BA on a part-time basis. Later, when the children were at school and Ian became Dean of Brisbane, she took a job in university administration, a field in which she remained for the next seventeen years. Her jobs were demanding and had a fair level of responsibility, continuing to distance her from her husband's ministry, she says.

'My husband always had an office outside the home and

spent long hours away from home, and so in some ways his commitment to his ministry (while of great benefit to the wider Church) had a negative impact on my life. My response was to make my own life of family and career.'

In addition to these tensions of ministry and marriage, Barbara found that adjusting to a new distant country took time. Over the years, she grew to love Australia. 'It is a land of great natural beauty with strange animals, huge birds, harsh deserts and lush rain forests. Its people are from many races, religions and national backgrounds and wrestle with the demands of this plurality. On a personal note, our life together in this place has had its share of joy, sorrow, anger and pain. Had it not been for our Christian faith we might not have continued together.'

The personal crisis which challenged, yet strengthened, that faith the most was the loss of their twenty-two-year-old son, Samuel, by his own hand. 'My husband, our daughter and I shared the hell of trying to reach out to and touch a depressed young man who had fallen under the influence of drugs, a young man we all loved so much but who could not allow that love to give him the strength to survive. During the time just before he died we, as a family, shared love, laughter and tears and sheer unadulterated terror. Others who have been close to someone on the verge of suicide will know what I mean.

'When trying to express how I feel about that time in our lives, I often use an image once used on a poster for an arts festival, a black and white photograph of a dirty old garbage can. Out of the garbage can is growing the only bit of colour in the picture, a brilliant, beautiful, pink rose. Our most terrible personal crisis was often like that. The hurt and the guilt and the emptiness remain, and always will I guess; but, as well, there is enriched love and joy in living – most unexpected gifts. We have been enriched as well as scarred and this naturally flows into the work we do,' she declares.

Not long after their son's death, Ian was elected Archbishop of Adelaide, his home diocese and the city of his birth. 'We were still grieving but our focus on new challenges kept the painful memories and haunting guilt from taking over, although they were always there and always will be there.'

The spiritual search of the grieving process propelled Barbara quite unexpectedly into studying theology. 'This has enriched my life beyond measure and provided a fulfilling way of bringing together my work experience and my life in the Church.'

Barbara is now registrar of a consortium of Anglican, Roman Catholic and Uniting Church theological colleges in Adelaide. 'Out of a time when life seemed a dark night of pain and loss has emerged the joy and light of a deepening spiritual awareness and the satisfaction of a career which complements my husband's calling.

'I feel truly blessed,' concludes Barbara.

Barbara's prayer

We pray for South Australians and for us all.

For our land

> We give thanks for
> azure sea and white hot sky,
> leafy Victorian streetscape vistas,
> miles of telegraph-pole-lined suburbs,
> serried ranks of grapevines,
> golden wheat under bluer sky,
> sheep, tin sheds, barking dogs,
> red dirt, stars, the dream time,
> and sky and more sky.

Barbara George – Australia

Hear our prayer

For the people

We pray that we may love one another:
the fresh-faced children of our bounty,
and the blank-eyed children of our neglect:
be they city, country, black, white,
Western, Asian, speakers of God,
speakers of not God or disciples of nothing,
all under that hot sky and more sky.

Hear our prayer

For all the world

We pray that we will love and be loved,
we children of a world of bounty, unspeakable joy,
smiles and eyes that weep with love;
yet a world of hollow-eyed hunger and pain,
unquenchable anger and inconsolable loss,
under a senseless sky.

We pray that we will find love in one another,
have courage to embrace our differences,
admit that we are no longer children shouting,
running, jumping, grabbing, holding,
and say, 'I love you because you are me and I am
    you and we are loved.'
We are grown up now, under a seamless sky.

Hear our prayer

Amen

Ian Jamieson – New Zealand

Fact file

Name: Ian William Andrew Jamieson
Date of birth: 4 October 1939
Wife: Penelope (Penny) Jamieson, Bishop of Dunedin,
  New Zealand
Children: Eleanor, Emily, Dorothy – all adults

Dunedin is an attractive city and port situated on the South Island of New Zealand. Founded in 1848 by an early Scottish explorer as a Scottish Free Church settlement, its very name, which is Gaelic for Edinburgh, breathes Scotland. It is an important industrial centre and has very good road, rail, air and sea connections. It is also noted for its green 'Town Belt', planned by the founders to surround the inner city with five hundred acres of forest. However, Dunedin will always stand out in my memory because the first visit could easily have been the last!

It was in 1987 that George and I made our first visit. Ian and Penny Jamieson were not living there then. We were in New Zealand for five weeks on a lecture tour with Anglican Renewal Ministries. Dunedin was the very last place we were to visit and we were very weary at the end of a gruelling schedule. We made an early start from Christchurch. It being winter, the weather was rather dull and misty, but we were looking forward to our time in Dunedin, especially as I had been told that I, as a Scot, would feel at home there! We were to stay with the bishop, going on at the end of our time there for a much-needed vacation in Honolulu, Vancouver and Toronto before we returned home. The flight from Christchurch was much the same as all the flights had been, and we had done many short hops. This particular plane was a Fokker Friendship 48. As the aircraft approached the runway, instead of landing it revved its engines deafeningly and gained instant height up over the ocean. We were all left holding our breath and panic-stricken, knowing that something had gone wrong. When we were on an even keel again the pilot announced that we had overshot the runway because of the fog; he would have one more attempt to land, but if that was not successful we would have to return to Christchurch. We were all somewhat apprehensive, but the second attempt was successful and a great cheer arose from the passengers when we were safely on the ground. Not an experience one easily forgets!

I had the pleasure of meeting Ian in August 1997 on an official visit to the diocese of Dunedin. He looked after my programme as any spouse of a bishop would do. He was terrific company and it seemed perfectly natural and no different from being with a female spouse.

Ian is like many of the spouses in this book who have careers of their own and have to juggle that with their commitment to a partner who has a very demanding role. However, he is particularly significant for this book. Penny, his wife, was the first woman diocesan bishop in the Anglican Communion. Therefore he is the first male spouse and rightly deserves a chapter.

The Bishop and I

Ian Jamieson

Ian Jamieson was the first diocesan bishop's husband in the Anglican Communion. He and Penny are of course used to hearing it being described the other way round. The disarming way he has come to terms with a role which for every clergy spouse has its problems is a model of good humour and understanding.

'I wish I knew,' he says, when asked to define his role. 'I think that the people of Dunedin were probably equally uncertain, if they gave it a thought among all the hype surrounding the decision of their electors to choose the first woman diocesan bishop anywhere. Would he come to church? Would he travel? Would he entertain? He obviously couldn't become president of the diocesan Association of Anglican Women. What would he do?'

Ian is quick to answer the question himself. 'I'm sure that I must "keep out of the way" in many areas. Women in this society have defeated, I'm glad to say, many gender expectations. But there still sometimes, and unexpectedly, lingers the expectation that the man really makes the decisions, even if now behind the scenes. It's there, even if only partly and apologetically, in the expectation once or twice expressed to me that I'll have "checked out" on a sermon before it's been given or that I know the confidential reasons behind a particular decision. I haven't and I don't, nor will I or should I.' He hopes that this is now widely known.

Like many other bishop's spouses he was initially more comfortable with the more accustomed role of being married to a parish priest. Penny was vicar of a parish in the diocese of Wellington before she moved to Dunedin. Ian ended up as a Sunday School teacher, as fourth relief organist, as a sidesperson, as mower of lawns and probably a number of things he would have been expected to do if he'd been a wife. He found that there were no expectations and he had much more freedom to choose than a woman in a comparable situation. There was even surprise, he recalls, that he went to church at all. 'We don't tend to have university people here . . .' was the explanation. But he found that in this parish there were 'more saints than any other parish in the country'. Ian's definition of a saint includes the necessity that the saint doesn't know it.

He accepts a deeply traditional role as a clergy spouse, to be supportive of his wife's ministry. When Penny was appointed Bishop of Dunedin in 1990, he had to give up his job as a senior member of the department of English at Victoria University of Wellington. Despite his explanation that he had become weighed down by administration and departmental politics, it cannot have been an easy thing to do. Yet, of course, this is a much more common 'choice' made by women. In Dunedin another job was to open up for him as a teaching fellow in English at the University of Otago. Here, to his relief, he can pursue his research and teaching of English literature. His specialisms are mediaeval literature, and twentieth-century Scottish literature – without the 'politics'.

'A bishop's life seems amazingly busy, in the range as well as the sheer number of commitments, and from time to time the complexity, as well as the unpleasantness and the destructiveness, of the issues with which bishops have to deal makes me wonder how they can sleep at night – sometimes they can't!'

On the practical side, he admits to not being able to cook, but happily they have a daughter still at home who can. 'But in most other ways, with the help of an admirable succession of cleaning ladies, I can try to keep the "daily round" tolerable, if not always thoroughly comfortable.'

He tries to travel with Penny within the diocese, sometimes driving her when she is visiting parishes, and he also travels overseas with her when it is a help to absorb at least some of the immense interest that a woman bishop attracts. He loves visiting parishes and feels that the way people welcome him has been a great gift to him personally, as now they realise that 'I am very ordinary, enjoy being part of a worshipping community, and don't need to have special arrangements made. Of course, the most useful way to be supportive is to be very happy and healthy myself,' he adds.

It already sounds as though, in addition to his half-time academic post, he does plenty as a bishop's spouse, but he is conscious of the need to gather clergy partners together more frequently. While they meet together once a year during synod, the distances are large, numbers are few, interests are diverse, and the demands of careers are often too great. 'And in some marriages,' he adds, 'both partners are ordained: so who is the spouse? But I do not want to excuse myself – there is more to be done.'

Ian acutely talks about a 'feeling of precariousness' when he describes southern New Zealand, where Penny's diocese is situated. The city of Dunedin itself, at the end of last century and the beginning of this, was a very wealthy and prospering financial and industrial centre. It was the discovery of gold inland in the province of Otago that brought wealth to the city, which, he says, was on the whole well spent. The first university in the country, the first secondary school for girls in the Southern Hemisphere, were built during these prosperous times. 'But that boom economy has now gone. The financial and industrial centres of New Zealand have moved to the North Island, especially to Auckland, and Dunedin and its hinterland feel exposed, sometimes even precarious.'

The main industry now in the city is centred on the

university, a polytechnic and a teacher training establishment. Southland, the second of the two provinces that comprise the diocese of Dunedin, is largely a farming community – one of the most fertile areas of the country. Now the farming industry shows signs of severe depression.

This feeling of 'precariousness' can also be applied to the Church. 'Since World War II, New Zealand has become one of the most secularised countries in the world. The trappings of civic importance are still there, especially in numbers of church buildings, but congregations have tended to become elderly and dwindling, and the significance of religious expression in civic life continues to decline.' Anglicans, he says, have noticed this decline as much as any other denomination. Whereas in the rest of the country Anglicanism was the majority faith, the south was a Presbyterian settlement. Roman Catholicism also is larger here than Anglicanism. 'In a number of congregations one senses a bewilderment as to how the faith can be passed on to the next generation.'

However, Ian does not tell a story of doom and gloom. 'One sees many determined signs of growth. In the economy there has been a big growth in tourism and in forestry, diversifying from traditional strengths but not shedding them.' And in the Church things are moving forward as well. He cites the move towards local ministry in small communities that can no longer afford to support traditional stipendiary ministry; the enthusiasm of young people in parishes which have a charismatic vocation; the example of a church that flourished because of the seriousness with which it undertook children's ministry, and parishes that have been 'loved to life' by the total commitment of a parish priest. 'Different parishes – different needs – different responses. There is no universal panacea. But behind it all, I guess, there is the care Anglicans always give to worship.'

Shared Anglican worship, with its aesthetic appeal to the heart and to the head, has always been at the heart of Ian's spirituality. His father was a grocer and both parents were very active members of a local Baptist church. Yet he recalls that his father's spirituality from his Anglican background made him something of a fish out of water. His mother had persuaded her husband that they needed to worship together for the good of the family and he entered into this commitment with determination, becoming a member of the deacon's court and the church secretary.

'The theological emphases of that community were "conversion" and "separation from the world", allied to an unexamined biblical fundamentalism. I went through the normal initiation rites of a young adolescent there – "conversion", "response to appeal for baptism" – as the appropriate emotional chords were played. But as I grew through my teens there, I felt increasingly alienated. My school enthusiasms were literature and language and history, and I was greatly influenced by a master whose life was surrounded by music (classical) and poetry. The particular cultural style and the scathingly anti-knowledge stridency of church "home" made me feel I did not belong. But that feeling I could, of course, not declare. The emotional bonds to the church group had their own pull, and the demands for loyalty at home were irresistible for a well-dominated adolescent. One learnt to live two lives.'

This, he says in retrospect, cannot have been healthy, but escape to university in another city provided a safety valve. There he remembers going through well-tried paths of 'snobbish scoffing, strutting and determined agnosticism' and 'intellectual superiority'. But he was never able to leave his Christian faith entirely behind. Instead he discovered the aesthetic pleasures of Anglican worship – the fine music and architecture and intelligent preaching. 'I rather "bathed" in that as a postgraduate student in the United Kingdom for those years in the early 1960s. I have since learnt, I hope, that worship is not about aesthetic pleasure but is rather (through God's grace) allowing oneself to be opened up into the glory and the demands of the presence of God.'

As he looks back on those early Baptist years he is at pains to point out that the level of community reliability, loyalty and self-denying service are values he still cherishes. His mother was an invalid for many years; because his father needed to remain at work, women from the church would look after his mother and sit with her.

He met Penny (who is English) when they were students at the University of Edinburgh for several years in the early 1960s. Penny was an undergraduate and Ian was a postgraduate and, for one year, a member of staff. The areas they worked in overlapped. Ian says, 'In those cosy days, there was much intermingling of students at different levels and, what was more to the point, Penny flatted in her final year with a New Zealand student who I knew well.' In the end, engagement and marriage happened very suddenly because Ian had to return to New Zealand to take up a position to which he was already contracted and to support his parents, struggling with illness. He goes on to say that he suspects it was only after marriage that they realised they 'had a lot in common (particularly religious needs) as well as a great deal of difference (for we come from entirely different family origins)'.

In the early 1970s, Ian had 'toyed' with the idea of a priestly vocation himself, until a wise priest gave him Henry Balmforth's book *Christian Priesthood* to read. It showed him immediately, he recalls, that he was totally unsuited.

Penny's call to the priesthood came later, in the mid 1970s. He claims that he was just back from retreat when Penny told him she was taking him out for dinner because she had something to tell him. He had already guessed what it was, and it seemed the easiest thing in the world to say, 'Go for it!' He goes on to say, 'To tell the truth, I felt at the time very privileged.'

Ian is a private sort of person who tends to shy away from opening up on personal issues, but throwing caution to the winds he says, 'I have had two quite severe bouts of depression in my life, though the really difficult times have not lasted more than a week or two. I thank God for medication and that I have never needed to be hospitalised.' Ian feels it may have made him more sympathetic, but actually can't see anything of value in it all. There have been other things too, but he guesses there are some lessons for 'ministry' in all of them.

The two traditions of Christianity from Ian's early life remain at the heart of his spirituality, where the community of the Church, the support and fellowship of each member and the sacramental signs of that community are of primary importance. 'I need to pray, in what's called "the very depths of my being", isn't it?

'I find I pray most naturally within the shapes provided by the liturgy of the Church. My normal pattern is to be at the Eucharist two or three times a week, and at Choral Evensong twice a week. I appreciate the particularity of each service – the round of festivals, the givenness of the readings. But I am also grateful for the orderedness and familiarity of the basic shapes into which one can pour all one's concerns and desperation, and sense that God's presence is there to absorb them – and even, occasionally, to make meaning out of confusion,' he declares.

Ian's prayer

Holy God,
We thank you for all the light, grace and life

Ian Jamieson – New Zealand

Seen and known in the Church that nurtures us.
Be with us in our life together in this diocese;
Open our eyes that we may recognise the work of
   your Spirit,
Among the dreams and visions of all your people.
Help us to leave yesterday
And not to covet tomorrow,
Accepting the uniqueness and the gift of today
As we engage in the mission of your Church.
Through Jesus Christ our Lord,

Amen

Najat Kafity – Israel

Fact file

Name: Najat Abed Kafity
Date of birth: 22 March 1940
Husband: Samir Kafity, Bishop of Jerusalem and the
  Middle East
Children: Two daughters: Samar, born 1965; Rula,
  born 1967

The land of Palestine has had a troubled history down
the ages. It has been controlled and ruled over the
last two thousand years by many different groups of
nationalities and religions: the Romans, Persians, Muslim
Arabs, Crusaders and finally the Turks for four hundred
years, prior to Palestine coming under mandatory British
control with the authority of the League of Nations in
1917. In 1948 the United Nations partitioned the country
between Israel and Jordan. A year later the state of Israel
was inaugurated.

In 1967 the Six Day War between Arabs and Jews
resulted in the Israeli occupation of the West Bank and
the Gaza Strip. Fighting for territory is still paramount
in this small country trying falteringly to keep the peace
process moving on. Palestinian and Jew want a homeland
and peoples of three religions – Christians, Jews and
Muslims – have a right to worship at their holy places.

Najat Kafity – Israel

There is a long way to go and many hurdles to be overcome before this can happen. George and I first went to Israel in 1975 with a group from St John's College, Nottingham, just before we moved to St Nicholas, Durham. We loved it and when an opportunity came to spend four months' sabbatical there in 1986 we jumped at the chance. Living in the land that Jesus lived in and walking where He walked brought our faith to life and gave a new reality to the Bible. Liz, our youngest daughter, was just fourteen at the time and it made a tremendous impression on her. When she married they chose to spend their honeymoon there.

We have been there several times since on official trips and have got to know Samir and Najat well. They have both been totally committed to the support of their own people, the Palestinians, and have risked much in their efforts for the peace process so that all the people in the Holy Land can have their rightful share of the land. It has not been easy for them and they have been very drained at times.

In March 1997 the Primates of the Anglican Communion met in Jerusalem at the invitation of Samir, and he arranged to take us all to the Gaza Strip, now the main centre of the Palestinian Authority. It was thrilling to see the way that Najat was acclaimed by the crowds who gathered to meet us. She responded naturally and warmly. She has had a truly caring ministry through all the troubles.

I am delighted that Najat has shared some of her experiences with us. I think in time she could tell us more, but she is too close to the situation at the moment and it is too painful. I am grateful that she has allowed us to enter into the pain of it with her.

The Bishop and I

Najat Kafity

Bishop Samir Kafity has been one of the most high-profile critics of injustice in the Anglican Communion. His role as Presiding Bishop of Jerusalem and the Middle East until 1996 gave him a special responsibility to speak up for the small Anglican community in Jerusalem, who had suffered alongside all the inhabitants of Israel and the Occupied Territories in the conflict between Israelis and Palestinians.

Samir's wife Najat has also had a key role to play alongside him in condemning injustice and speaking up for those who are not usually heard. It is not surprising that she has strong feelings. 'The story of the people of Jerusalem diocese is the story of peace and justice,' she says. 'Justice was not done to the Palestinians, while for the last fifty years it was our plea. While Israel was nourished and supported by many Christians in the world, people in my diocese felt betrayed and forgotten.

'My life and my thinking were affected by all the politics of the Middle East. I wanted a just solution but there are no one hundred per cent solutions, so we compromise, accept and make the best of it.

'We are waiting for the birth of Palestine in a couple of years. The people of this diocese will have time to rest spiritually and physically. Hopefully then we can witness in a relaxed way without fear and anger,' she declares. Despite years of conflict in the land of her birth, her optimism about the future is great. She believes that one of the main tests for Christians is whether they will be willing to abide by the New Testament teaching concerning enemies and neighbours.

'I often wonder about this one God that all of us worship – a God in whose name we go to war. We lose our lands and our homes. and some of our children get killed. Others become terrorists and extremists. What is the true God?' she asks. 'How can we accept a God who deprives us of a home? What a challenge to turn hearts of bitterness to love, acceptance and respect. What is the formula? I don't know. My best answer is to start with my own self and within my family. May God be my helper and redeemer.'

Najat was born into an Anglican family in Nablus. Her father went to Bishop Gobat's School in Jerusalem and was enriched by the Anglican tradition. He held management posts during the British mandate. Her mother went to St Margaret's School in Nazareth; although she came from an Orthodox background, a Protestant theology was instilled in her school years. Najat's parents were married in 1939 in Nablus and had seven children, five girls and two boys. While the rest of the family emigrated to the United States after the Six Day War in 1967, Najat was already married to Samir and living in Beirut.

'My Christian faith to me was a serious thing, not just to talk about but to live. Our Sunday School classes were held on Friday, the Muslim day off. Being a minority didn't give me any problem. My friends were Muslims. I knew culturally what they did and they knew about my faith.' While Najat recognised that there was a cultural element to each religion, like the Christmas tree or Easter eggs or special sweets and parties for some of the Muslim festivals, the one cultural trapping which she was unhappy to accept was the perception of Christianity as a Western faith. 'I'm part and parcel of this society, although we do things differently.' The question of identity is a major issue for the Christian Arab. Anglicans have gone to great lengths to ensure that liturgies and biblical texts are in Arabic, so that their faith can no longer be perceived as a Western and alien faith. In contrast, the truth is, of course, that Christianity finds its beginnings in the Holy Land.

Both Najat and Samir's families lived in Nablus, and their fathers worked together on church committees. Samir used to give the young Najat Sunday School classes (on Fridays) and organise the youth group when he was home from college.

'We enjoyed having him around,' she remembers. 'He was a good organiser and good company. We were all about fourteen or fifteen years old and he was twenty-two. Days and years went by and we went down our own paths. I went to the States and came back in 1961. Samir was then a priest in Ramallah. A young priest needs to find a bride,' she explains. 'The late Bishop Cubain and Samir's parents pushed for this match and it happened.

'I wasn't in love or romantic. Wise people think that love comes afterwards and so it did. My daughters think that this is the old-fashioned way. Maybe so. I think that a compatible marriage and a marriage in two families that know each other is a part of our culture,' she says simply.

At the beginning Najat really did not want to be married to a priest. She took some convincing. At the time she was not deeply interested in the Bible, neither did she have a disciplined way of prayer. Even going to church every Sunday was difficult, when her day off was Friday. It was too much of a commitment, she admits. 'But now, after thirty-three years of marriage, I have my own faith, which negates many things of traditional theology. But it was Samir's charm, personality and generosity which surpassed my scepticism. The decision was made and here we are, grandparents to three lovely children,' she says proudly.

On the positive level, she has found that being married to a priest has opened up a whole sphere of new life. Najat has been with Samir in meeting many people, the young, old, rich, poor and sick. It has given her a spectrum of human experiences which she has valued. It has enabled her to think deeply about humanity in its strength and weakness and appreciate the diversity and common things in God's creation. 'Attitudes', she discovered, 'can be changed.'

'Negatively, as I grow older, I am getting less tolerant. I have become sensitive to hypocrisy and double standards and I find the world is full of it. Being exposed to a wide world, whether it is in the Church or outside, is shaking my expectations. Maybe I shouldn't expect too much of people ordained or not ordained. Knowing a lot of inside politics in the Church isn't something that I like,' she says.

Najat describes her role as a 'supportive one', but she has also asserted herself, thereby 'preserving' her own personality and identity. 'As a bishop's wife, lately I find myself alone doing what other women do, visiting and inviting people to my home. I travel for family purposes, for example when my father was sick, or when a daughter is due to deliver.'

But, she argues, being related to someone who has authority causes isolation. 'Decisions taken by a bishop might anger people and cause uncomfortable relationships. As a wife, some feel that I am part of his decision and react against me. So my social circle gets smaller and more cautious. Somehow I pay a price,' she says.

Above all, Najat says that she doesn't assume a special role as a bishop's wife. She says that one of the best compliments she has received was when a friend said simply, 'We don't feel that you are a bishop's wife.'

Najat's prayer

God of peace and love, we pray for the ministry of our diocese, that you may grant peace to all those who live in this land;

For love, harmony and reconciliation;

For wisdom, that we may understand the diversity of your creation;

To rediscover and revive the holiness of the Holy Land among Jews, Christians and Muslims as we all worship one loving God.

Amen

Madeleine Kayumba – Rwanda

Fact file

Name: Madeleine Uzabakiriho Kayumba
Date of birth: 26 April 1955
Husband: Norman Kayumba, Bishop of Kigeme, Rwanda
Children: One daughter, Angela; three sons, Ammiel,
  Joshua and Emmanuel
First language: Kinyarwanda

I first met Madeleine in December 1994 in Nairobi, Kenya.
We were on an official visit to the Church of the province
of Kenya. The bishops and their spouses of the province of
Rwanda came for an important breakfast meeting with my
husband and his staff at our hotel. The dreadful genocide
in Rwanda had started on 6 April of that year. Close to a
million men, women and children had been systematically
killed in this almost unbelievable ethnic conflict which had
stunned the world and left it feeling powerless. Many of the
bishops had fled from the country with their families. Some
had gone back, but others were too frightened.

We then visited the country of Rwanda in May the
following year. The devastation caused by what had
happened was still in evidence all around us. We were in
the midst of a country in a state of shock. A country that
had once been beautiful and civilised was now a country
of orphans and widows. There were huge numbers of relief

organisations from many different countries trying to bring some order to the chaos, but they, along with the newly formed government, were starting with nothing in this country that had literally destroyed itself.

Norman, Madeleine's husband, was one of the bishops who stayed with his people in his diocese and protected and saved many of them. We visited the diocese of Kigeme and saw some of the rebuilding of lives and living conditions that he was achieving with the help of others. It is a very poor area of Rwanda; before the genocide the people were only scratching an existence from the very poor soil and many of them were suffering from malnutrition even then.

One of my great treasures is a poster I was given in Rwanda by the government Minister for Women and Children. She was a lovely young woman who graciously agreed to see me and tell me about the work she was trying to do in very difficult circumstances. Her office was very bare, but on the wall was this one poster.

It was not in a frame but my eyes kept straying to it and I felt it was drawing me like a magnet. It showed two poorly clad children, about five or six years old, trying to scrape the soil with a very crude farming implement. They were looking towards me, with the barren countryside in the background, and in their eyes shone hope. My heart lifted within me and I too saw hope. Hope for this country will come with the youngsters wanting a better life and 'putting their shoulders to the plough'.

Madeleine is studying at St Paul's Theological College in Limuru, Kenya. She's an able theologian and feels called to these further studies, despite the pain of being away from home and especially from her husband. But she is going to use her gifts and the skills she is learning in the vital task of empowering women for ministry when she returns. She longs to be back in Rwanda with Norman and among their people, working with him, when her studies are completed.

This chapter must have been very painful for Madeleine to write but I am so glad that she has done it. We need to know the pain in the hearts of the people of Rwanda.

Madeleine Kayumba

In April 1994 the country of Rwanda hit the international headlines. It rapidly emerged from hourly newscasts that we were witnessing not the breakdown of a democratic system, but instead one of the most horrific ethnic conflicts ever seen. Here is not the place to relate again the terrible violence of which humans are capable of inflicting upon one another, but to listen to one woman's experience of growing through pain and guilt.

Norman was appointed Bishop of Kigeme in 1992. There was hardly time to get used to the office before the fateful events broke out. During the killing the Church was scattered. Madeleine explains: 'Many of those who needed our care were killed. We did not manage to protect many. I just feel inadequate.'

Her words are punctuated with the grief and guilt that many Christians feel about the genocide. Her husband, Norman, sheltered the Anglican Church's only Tutsi bishop, Alexis, during the genocide, risking death himself from the gangs of Hutus who scoured the countryside in the tribal slaughter. At an international gathering of Anglicans, Bishop Norman humbled the communion with his words from the Church in his country:

We Christians of Rwanda are indeed ashamed. We do repent and apologise before you all and ask you to please take that message to the whole world. We are ashamed of what you saw and are still seeing from our country, on your television screens. We have given non-believers another reason to resist God, because they thought that if such atrocities could be committed in a country where more than 80 per cent of the population is said to be Christian, that the message of that faith has been grossly contradicted.

He continued:

But let me tell you, brothers and sisters, that God is and has been all the time working in Rwanda in spite of our having failed Him in this way. We see God working through those who are willing to be used by Him and who are not ashamed at all before God. We have good testimonies of how Christians have used all that was available to them to help others in need and to resist the plan of the devil as they could. Today, we face very strong and hard challenges and we think that this is a lesson maybe intended by God to help other nations, so that they would not be surprised by what surprised us last year.

Madeleine is one of ten children. Her father, Bernard, was divorced twice before he married her mother, Theresa. Neither of his previous wives had borne him children and Madeleine believes that is why he did not stay with them, but her parents stayed together for the rest of their lives.

The family practised both Christian and traditional faiths simultaneously. Madeleine says, 'We would pray together as a family in the morning and before bed, but we would turn to ancestor worship in times of calamities or making important decisions.' She says that this did not disturb her at all because she thought there were just different ways of worshipping one God.

After finishing primary school and going to an Anglican

school in Kigeme, Madeleine says she was induced to revolt because of the inequality that she found among the pupils at the school. She says, 'Some were rich and others poor like us, and I accused God of being partial in His judgments.' This stopped her from asking to be baptised when she went home.

There was a spiritual revival at her school in Kigeme in 1970 following a crisis between Hutu and Tutsi girls. Madeleine says, 'I was among the last to respond, but on 17 January 1970, I confessed my sins, was prayed for and believed I was born again.' She goes on to say, 'I received two gifts of the Spirit, love and joy, and eight months later was baptised and received into the Baptist Church.'

This was the beginning of a long journey for Madeleine, ending in her meeting Norman at a Scripture Union camp in 1972. He was already studying theology and she was an evangelist – it just seemed perfect. But, Madeleine says, 'I had to change my denomination because the bishop said a pastor and his wife had to be the same, so I became an Anglican.'

Madeleine found her life was very different being married to a pastor. First, she had to follow Norman wherever he was called to serve, therefore having to change her job frequently; second, her timetable changed. She says, 'Though I enjoyed company, I also liked to be alone and found I was expected to be available all the time for people.' Although Madeleine found it hard to meet all the challenges, by God's grace she did her best.

The pain of being scattered by the violence is something Madeleine feels very strongly. She started writing theological books in 1990, first *The Women of the Bible* and then *The Bride of Christ*. It was in order to pursue this that she began studying theology in Nairobi, Kenya. She now feels torn between the immediate needs of her country and husband and what she feels is her calling to study theology for ministry when she returns. She says, 'Our diocese is located in the poorest area of our country. Most of our Christians do not have the necessary food, clothes and shelter. Sometimes, I find myself just useless! I cannot assist many. I am really helpless.' More than half the population are illiterate, and the war destroyed the efforts of the government and the diocese to teach reading, especially to adults.

Women have responded powerfully to the situation in Rwanda. The Mothers' Union has had a mini-revival in most parishes. In Kenya, Madeleine receives letters from Mothers' Union members, and she looks forward to joining them in their work to strengthen families in Rwanda.

'In this time of disintegration of the society, traditional values (such as hospitality and mutual assistance) are being lost. However, I realised that people expect to find them in the minister's homes, especially in bishops' families. The common saying that "the woman is the heart of the family" (*umugore ni umutima w'urugo*) applies also to the bishop's wife. When the husband's ministry is blessed, the bishop's wife should expect more people home and be available,' Madeleine says.

For the last ten years, Madeleine has also had to contend with ill health and high blood pressure which has worsened as a result of the war. At first she did not take it seriously, and with a strong belief in divine healing failed to take any medicine, except valium from time to time. 'However, slowly but surely this sickness affected my temperament. Sometimes I would be very tired and nervous, other times very cheerful, other times depressed. The problem is that some people who have heard me preach or read my books do not always find in me all the charisma they expect. It is frustrating. However, many understand and help me. This sickness has helped me to grow and experience the concern of other people. It has also increased my own concern for those who go through difficulties.' Madeleine now has to spend a great deal of money on medicines and has had to accept that she cannot be available to everyone who needs her.

Yet she nevertheless expresses a great deal of frustration. 'There are conflicting demands on my time,' she admits. 'I feel that now I am a student, a mother, a bishop's wife, I am not performing well in any of all these important responsibilities.

'As a student, I am very busy with classes, papers to write and exams to prepare. As a mother, I need to spend time with my children, teach them cooking, read their homework and have leisure time together, but sometimes I can't even do that. Even our family prayers are not regular. As a pastor's wife, I need to have time for my husband, pray with him, and share his joys and worries. And since he lives in Rwanda, we try to make the little time we have together "quality time", but we can't. And since we are here to serve, we also minister to other people. Now that their needs have increased, we are literally submerged,' Madeleine says.

This cry for help is born out of Madeleine's feelings of powerlessness. Yet she sets her sights high, believing that it is her responsibility to extend Christian love and hospitality to all people. 'In this time of crisis in our country, I find that a bishop's wife has a tremendous responsibility towards widows and orphans. She must be a model in ministering to people from different ethnic groups. She needs to build bridges.'

Madeleine's prayer

Lord, my heart is full of praises.
I praise you for choosing me and anointing me.
Who am I, Lord?

The Bishop and I

You put me closer to your servant, Bishop Norman,
And I know him more than anybody else.

Lord, help me to be the mate he really needs,
To value this privilege
And assume this responsibility,
For your own glory.

But Lord, my heart is also bleeding.
Norman is in Rwanda, and I am here in Kenya.
Part of the flock is in Rwanda, the other outside.
Some bishops are inside, others outside.

Lord, can't you gather us together again
For the glory of your Name
And the good of your Church?

Lord, I remain open to you and to your people.
I want to see,
To see people as you see them
And help Norman to 'oversee'.
I want my heart to open widely
Wide enough to accommodate all,
both Hutus and Tutsis.

Lord, I beseech you.
Forgive our sins and heal our wounds,
Assist us in our struggle for reconciliation,
Bless our efforts.

Assist all bishops' wives in the world
To be genuine co-workers,
To grow together with their husbands,
For the glory of your Name and the good of
   your people.

Madeleine Kayumba – Rwanda

Help us to be continually crucified with you,
To continually rise up along with you,
To assume our duties and responsibilities
With the Risen Christ,
Through the power of the Holy Spirit.

Amen

Rachel Leake – Argentina

Fact file

Name: Rachel Leake
Date of birth: 15 July 1940
Husband: David Leake, Bishop of the diocese of Argentina
Children: Andrew, 35, married to Maria Mercedes with a son and a daughter; Philip, 32, married to Victoria; Judith, 30, married to Ken

George and David both trained at the London College of Divinity in Northwood. David was ahead of George, but they overlapped by a year. So the connections we have with David go back a long way. But I was only to meet Rachel many years later.

The diocesan see for the whole of South America where David and Rachel work was originally on the Falkland Islands. It was later transferred to the city of Buenos Aires in Argentina, from where the bishop made extraordinarily lengthy pastoral journeys all over South America. The cathedral in that city dates back to 1831 and was the first non Roman Catholic church building in South America.

David was made a bishop when he was very young, but then the Anglican Church in South America is very young also. It was only in 1969 that the vast country of Argentina was split up into two dioceses and David became an assistant bishop in the diocese of Northern Argentina. He and Rachel were there until 1989 when he was elected to become diocesan bishop of Argentina.

I first met Rachel at the 1989 Lambeth Conference. My lasting memory is the great love and care she gave to the Spanish-speaking wives. Most of them had no English and throughout the main sessions she 'whisper' translated for them. Anyone who has done that will know how exhausting it is, particularly over a period of three weeks. It meant that she could not fully benefit from the conference herself.

Thankfully Rachel will be able to participate fully in the 1998 Lambeth Conference, where simultaneous translation is planned for the spouses' programme.

Rachel Leake

'The South Atlantic War in 1982 proved to be a tense period for us,' says Rachel, 'especially for those with strong ties in England, yet with a life commitment to Argentina. We received written threats on our lives, but thankfully nothing came of them. We remained in Argentina throughout the war, although we had to make arrangements for British members of the diocesan staff to be evacuated to Paraguay.'

For the last thirty-four years Rachel Leake has lived in Argentina, married to David who was first a missionary priest, then a bishop and for a time presiding bishop of the Southern Cone of South America. She was born in a small fishing town in Norfolk, in the east of England, in 1940.

She describes her parents as 'God-fearing'. Her father was strict but very loving, demanding on himself and self-disciplined. He expected his children to follow his own good example in everything. He had been used to responsibility early, taking over as man of the house when his own father died at a young age from drowning, while saving some swimmers. 'My father had great perseverance and high moral standards and was, with his very enquiring mind, a lover of culture, justice and nature. He prepared us for the future with great thoughtfulness and self-sacrifice and encouraged us to go out and about, always being available at his desk to help us in any way and encourage us to learn,' she says.

Her mother also left an abiding impression which was to guide Rachel in her own choices throughout her life. Rachel describes her as 'selfless', 'hardworking' and 'self-effacing'. She went about her work helping her husband with cheerfulness and optimism and a wonderful sense of humour. 'Mum was always ready to listen with sympathy and understanding and with encouraging words when necessary. She kept an open home and was always constant and available to give us love and advice and to show by example how to live for others and to put them first.'

Despite the fact that it was wartime, Rachel has happy memories of a stable childhood with her brother and sister. 'There was rationing and second-hand clothes, Red Cross parcels at school from the States, moving from home using a wheelbarrow, playing bombs inside the air-raid shelter, and then the joy of queuing up for unrationed sweets and the car being returned, which I didn't know we possessed!

'I have memories of cycling the three miles to school on bitterly cold days getting chapped knees and hands, as well as wonderful memories of long idyllic days on the beach, magical Christmases with real candles at dangerous angles on real Christmas trees.' Sunday, she remembers, was special because it was the only day when they had tea in the living room and when her father was not in his office.

The stability and security continued throughout her teenage years, but she remembers that the high standards and demands were not always easy. The young Rachel was nervous sometimes at school because she could not always do as well as expected; a particular mathematics teacher caused her great anxiety. Yet she recalls gaining tremendous security from knowing exactly what her father would be doing at certain times because of his systematic lifestyle. He would help all his children with their homework, looking things up for them in an amazing filing system in shoe boxes all over the house. 'Never do I remember wanting to rebel against my parents in any serious way. Life was good and home was often full of interesting, colourful visitors from many places, which was a great preparation for the future,' she says.

The stability of her home also provided a context of Christian love, in which she says she was always 'conscious of the name and presence of Jesus'. One of the early memories that sticks out in her mind was that of seeing her parents in prayer. She went to a Methodist Sunday School twice each Sunday from the age of four. As well as church attendance, there were bedtime prayers and grace at meal times. Family prayers began when she was in her teens. At the age of eight, Rachel saw a film on leprosy work which kindled an ambition to become a missionary nurse. Every Sunday she collected money from neighbours for the Methodist Missionary Society and stored sixpenny pieces in a phial. Twenty-one shillings covered a year's treatment for a leper. Whenever there was an evangelistic 'campaign' in town, she would go. She also remembers responding each time to the altar call to follow Jesus. Maybe this was to please the speaker, she now speculates. One day her mother came to her bed and said, very gently, 'Rachel, if you already have Jesus in your heart you don't need to keep standing up – He's already there!'

But the famous evangelist Billy Graham, who preached at Haringey in London in the 1950s, had an enduring influence on her plans. 'I realised that all my plans for the future were my own plans and that I needed to know God's plan for my life, so went forward to rededicate my life to Him and to get things into the right perspective.'

Eventually the family joined the Anglican Church, where her sister and brother had for some time been members of the choir. There was very little life or teaching in the church, but Rachel was able to join a local interdenominational group where she met her future husband, David.

David was born and brought up in Northern Argentina by his missionary parents, who worked among the Toba and Mataco Indians. The family returned to England in 1954 so that David and his two sisters could carry on their education in Britain. Rachel's first glimpse of David was at a meeting when he was putting slides of the missionary work in Northern Argentina into the projector for his uncle. Despite the fact that he managed to get them upside down, they began to get to know each other better.

A friendship began between the two families when Rachel was fourteen, but it was not until she was seventeen that she began to go out with David. 'I was still at school then and David was at the London College of Divinity in Northwood, Middlesex. David had already felt the call to become a priest before we began to go out together, and to me it was a real privilege and challenge to join him in this wonderful calling,' she says.

By the time they married, Rachel had completed her nursing training at Addenbrooke's Hospital in Cambridge and David had been a curate at St Mary's, Watford, for two years. Although Rachel had planned to carry on with her nursing career, she quickly began to find the working hours incompatible with David's, so gave up work and began to visit in the parish and help out where the needs were.

During this period of her life, she began to experience a feeling of isolation. Having left the nursing friends with whom she had lived, and with David being out during the day and often in the evenings, she says, 'There was a sudden loss of set work and responsibilities and I was expecting a baby. These feelings affected me and also David adversely. It must have been unsettling for him. I feel that there had not been any proper preparation for entering this new life as a curate's wife.'

In 1963 the couple and their little son Andrew went out to live in northern Argentina among the Indians. They were to find a very different life in this beautiful country. Argentina is divided into the diocese of Northern Argentina, to the north, and the diocese of Argentina, with its diocesan centre in Buenos Aires, of which David has been bishop for seven years after twenty-seven years in the northern diocese. He was consecrated bishop in the North in 1969. Both dioceses cover enormous distances. In the diocese of Argentina itself, about a thousand people worship on Sundays. Recently David and Rachel travelled a distance the equivalent of London to Istanbul to visit small scattered groups living on estancias, for baptisms and annual services. These vast distances make it very difficult to build up people in the Christian faith and give them a sense of continuity and belonging.

The Anglican Church began as chaplaincy churches when the British were building the railways. They were intended to meet the spiritual needs of the expatriate British. As a result, all the services were in English, with the notable exception of one Anglican church led by William Case Morris (often referred to as the Dr Barnardo of South America) who in the early 1900s cared for thousands of children as well as establishing an Argentine Spanish-speaking Anglican church. Unfortunately, this initiative was not continued after his death. It was only twenty-five years ago that special efforts were made to establish Spanish-speaking work alongside the English. Those of an older generation found this change very difficult and so a service in English is still held in most of the churches. This does mean that there is not always unity between the groups.

'Economically things are difficult too,' Rachel says. 'This diocese is almost one hundred per cent self-financed and this means that we cannot afford to have more clergy. Often at the end of the month one wonders where the support for the clergy is going to come from. The cost of living in Argentina is very high.'

Nevertheless, the Anglican Church continues to seek more opportunities for service. There are two day-care centres and other work among the many poor and needy of Argentina. Other plusses, she says, are the opportunities for ministry among the women, with quiet days and Bible study and prayer groups in the churches of the diocese. Marriage Encounter weekends go from strength to strength, she reports. There is also work with street people. Furthermore, people are offering themselves for ordination and even for non-stipendiary ministry. 'I believe that the size of the diocese, and of the city in general, gives a sense of constant struggle and the feeling of facing an impossible task. One sometimes feels envious of the apparent numerical success of other churches (e.g. the Pentecostals). It is easy in a country where there has been a history of corruption and injustice to get this into one's system and to think that nothing can change, but here and there we are seeing miracles where God is working and changing lives. It gives me great joy to see the women after a quiet day, to see people grow in their Christian faith and to see the deep commitment of those people offering for ordination.'

Thrown into a different culture and into the demanding role of being a priest's and then a bishop's wife, Rachel is full of humility. 'I have learnt that it is of the utmost importance to keep close to God. I can do nothing in my own strength. Leadership can be lonely and vulnerable and one does need to be encouraged and supported. I am aware that I am just a very ordinary person, and that above all else we need to do everything in love and with love that comes from above.'

Rachel finds the strength she needs for each day from sharing and praying with her husband. She also meets regularly with the wife of a local Presbyterian minister for times of prayer. 'The longer I go on the more I realise that the most important source of spiritual strength is from a real and personal close fellowship with God. I find the best time is at the beginning of each day, but this is not always easy, especially when there are visitors and when I feel tired. However, if I am disciplined, this is the best thing.'

Rachel's prayer

Dear Gracious Father,

Thank you because you are working throughout this diocese in many different ways. Please keep David and Rachel very close to yourself, and give them discipline to spend time with you and to watch for what you are doing and to listen to your voice so as to know your will.

We pray that you will move there among your people, bringing them to sacrificial commitment and a deep love that reaches out to people of all sections of society and removes their complacency.

We pray for your blessing and grace upon all the congregations scattered throughout that vast and beautiful country.

Thank you, God, for all you have done and all you will do in the future. In the name of Jesus,

Amen

Olga Lindsay – West Indies

Fact file

Name: Olga Daphne Lindsay
Date of birth: 13 July 1932
Husband: Orland Ugham Lindsay, Bishop of the diocese
   of the North Eastern Caribbean and Aruba (formerly
   Antigua) and Archbishop of the West Indies from 1986
Children: Richard, 36; Howard, 33; Jonathan, 26

When my husband was asked to become Archbishop
of Canterbury I had considerable worries about the
implications of such a move. At lunch one day in a
Roman Catholic study centre, I found myself sitting next
to Rabbi Lionel Blue, who is a well-known writer and
broadcaster in England, and I mentioned my hesitations
to him. His response was typical and delightful. 'Eileen,'
he said, 'imagine your new role like a box of chocolates.
There are the ones that are your favourites, others that you
like if the favourites have gone and some that you don't like
very much at all. Imagine your new life like that, picking
up one marked "places of beauty" or "interesting people",
perhaps "exciting adventures", and you will be able to face
life with confidence.'

I have never forgotten Lionel's way of helping me to
look positively at what lay ahead. That is a good way of
introducing my next contributor. Surely there can be few

more beautiful places than the West Indies, lying like a string of pearls in the Caribbean Sea.

I first met Olga in Newcastle, Northern Ireland, at the Primates' Meeting in 1991 when George was Archbishop-designate, just before he was enthroned in Canterbury Cathedral on 19 April. Olga's husband, Orland, was Archbishop of the West Indies and had been since 1986. All the Primates and their spouses were present to support George at that magnificent service. I have met Olga several times since at similar occasions and we have become good friends.

The island of Antigua, now known as Aruba, covers 108 square miles. It is one of the larger West Indian islands and has a mean annual temperature of 81°F with very little variation from month to month. All the islands lie in the path of the seasonal hurricanes. Tourism and agriculture are the main occupations. The language spoken is English and the vast majority of the population are Christians, with the Anglican Church predominant. This island is where Archbishop Orland and Olga live and he is diocesan bishop.

We paid a very short visit to Barbados, one of the other islands, in 1995 for celebrations to mark the 250th anniversary of Codrington College, which was the first college to train men for the priesthood in the Anglican Communion. Orland, as archbishop, was due to host us with Olga and the Bishop of Barbados but there had been devastating hurricanes just prior to our arrival. Their diocese had been very badly damaged and they rightly stayed with their people. We were sad not to see them but they were needed desperately to help alleviate the suffering of many people who had lost everything.

Olga's story will give you a glimpse into her life and a better understanding of what it is like to live in an area that is threatened frequently by natural disasters.

The Bishop and I

Olga Lindsay

Orland's call to be Bishop of Antigua in 1970 was a major jolt in Olga's life. Although born of Jamaican parents in Cuba, Olga had lived since the age of four in Jamaica and her husband's priestly calling had always been served close to home.

'Bishop Gibson, the then Bishop of Jamaica, had a lot of confidence in him. He had been sent to be the first local chaplain of the Jamaica Defence Force after Jamaica's independence. He also became the first Jamaican principal of Church Teachers' College in 1967,' she explains. 'The college had 300 students, 250 of whom were in residence. It was almost like a small parish with him as the priest in residence. Mandeville is a beautiful town, with lush green vegetation, and we were comfortable there.'

Her only sight of Antigua was in transit shortly before. The airport had seemed dingy and the surrounding area dry and barren. It did not pose an attractive picture. The questions came flooding: 'What would happen to our parents, who were getting older? Would the children suffer from the move?' Furthermore, the clergy in Jamaica did not want to see Orland leave and their counterparts in Antigua had experienced problems in choosing their new bishop. These factors were to leave Orland and Olga feeling very apprehensive.

Letters from Antigua quickly persuaded the couple to change their minds. One came from Dr C.E.S. Bailey, a high-ranking member of the cathedral, and another from a woman in the diocese. Both letters bore almost the same plea: 'There is plenty of work to do – come and help us.' And so they set course for Antigua.

Becoming a bishop's wife immediately changed the course of Olga's life and was to prove valuable preparation for the time when Orland was chosen to be Archbishop of the West Indies sixteen years later. For a start, Olga decided to give up work and remain at home. As well as supporting Orland in the many tasks he performed, she did all the cooking and household chores for a family with three strapping sons. In addition, she says that until recently, with the diocese on a firmer footing, she did all the cooking for synods and clergy retreats and meetings at Bishop's Lodge, with some help from a few ladies of the parish. She has no regrets: 'I think my being an anchor at home has contributed to our family being very close knit.'

Olga treasured the stabilising role of her own mother and grandmother. Her father, from Jamaica, met her mother in Cuba after he had migrated there in search of work in the sugar industry. Twin sisters came first, then Olga, another sister and a brother. But only Olga and her brother survived in a time when the infant mortality rate was much higher than today.

Olga's father took up his trade as a licensed plumber when the family returned to Jamaica. He spent much time in search of work, travelling to North America on a farming scheme and then trying his luck in England during the Jamaican migration to the UK in the 1950s.

'My only brother was sent to live in the country with my aunt who had no children. I remember being at home with my grandmother and mother very often. My grandmother and I shared a room. I can still remember the vast amount of patience she showed during the illness of her last years. They both became the stable influence in my life. I remember being very afraid of my father, who was a strict disciplinarian. If I was playing on the sidewalk outside our house I remember watching out for him and running inside when I saw him coming home.'

Nevertheless, Olga says her childhood was quiet and uneventful. Her mother was not always very well and consequently from the age of about fourteen she assumed many of the responsibilities for household duties.

Her passage through school to complete the Cambridge Junior and Senior Examinations was made possible through the insistence of her godmother, her mother's first cousin, known as Dear Ma. Olga remembers fondly: 'She had a clear vision for our lives. She was a talented dressmaker and sewed for many middle-class people. There were two other girls, one the daughter of an uncle and the other a great-niece of my grandmother, who lived with us for some time. She insisted that we should all learn to sew. She literally forced my family to send me to high school. I think she was also responsible for the financial aspect of it, for my father was not particularly mindful about such things. I can remember spending some lovely happy holidays with a second godmother in the country. She loved me very much and was very kind to me.'

After high school at the Rollingtown Government School and later the Camperdown High School for Girls, Olga registered at a commercial school in East Kingston for a nine-month book-keeping, shorthand and typing course. She didn't like the book-keeping and dropped it after three weeks. But something must have rubbed off, she laughs, for her subsequent career was as an accounts clerk.

The focus of her mother's life was the Anglican Church, and so Olga grew up in the Church. She went to Sunday School and eventually became a Sunday School teacher. She also joined the Anglican Young People's Association and subsequently became president of the branch at her church, All Saints.

'As I look back, I realise that there were not very many friends in my life and very few apart from these religious activities that I was involved in,' she says with disarming honesty. But it was such religious activities that brought her together with Orland. They met at an AYPA camp held at Montego Bay in August 1957. She was responsible for a group of young people from All Saints while Orland was one of the chaplains.

The typically strict rules of the camp included the stipulation that lights were to be out by 9 p.m. Olga continues: 'The young people had been cooped up for the better part of two weeks participating in lectures and discussions, and on their last evening I gave in to their requests for an end-of-camp party, provided that they kept their noise levels low.' Her first meeting with her husband-to-be therefore was not very promising. 'As chaplain, he came to demand why the rules were being broken, and I naturally felt obliged to defend the young people. At the time, he was also suffering from the effects of a bad flu and I offered him medication.'

Their next meeting was by accident on a bus later in the year, when Olga was returning from work. Orland was then teaching at Kingston College and was soon to be ordained as a deacon. A friendship gradually developed despite the unpromising start, and they were married in January 1959.

'When Orland asked me to marry him, by now I knew that I loved him and wanted to marry him but I was still apprehensive as to whether I was making the right decision. I didn't have anyone to talk to about our relationship. Although I had a brother I was brought up as an only child and in a very sheltered environment where the sharing of deep personal feelings had not been encouraged.

'I remember the day when I told my mother that Orland and I had been friends and he had asked me to marry him. I have thought many times since that I would never want my own children to experience what I went through in making the decision,' she declares.

For one thing she was scared about measuring up to

the demands that might be expected of her. She felt that she was not 'someone for a social life' and could not see herself in a public-speaking role. It was the 'holier than thou' role that put her off being a parson's wife. With the passage of time she can now say simply: 'I am grateful that Orland never forced me into doing anything that I didn't feel comfortable about.'

She soon found that being married to a priest gave her immense opportunities to grow personally, spiritually and emotionally, although she has had to 'make do' with very little materially. Furthermore, when Orland became a bishop a constant stream of visitors to Bishop's Lodge meant that she developed a much greater confidence. 'Orland's ministry has given me the opportunity to travel regionally and internationally. Under normal circumstances, these opportunities might not have been afforded me.'

Now, Olga gives much of her time to the children, young adults and women of the diocese. After serving as vice president, in 1996 she became president of the St John's Day Nursery Board. The nursery serves thirty to forty-five children in a low income area of St John's, the capital of Antigua. She is also a member of the executive of the Antigua and Barbuda Girl Guides' Association. This has involved her in fund-raising efforts to carry on the work of the Association and to help rebuild the headquarters. Such fund-raising efforts have also led her on to the planning committee to build a home for the elderly, an initiative by Anglican clergy.

Like many bishops' wives in various parts of the world she is also involved with the Mothers' Union. She is diocesan treasurer and meets once a month with the island council.

But one of the most satisfying experiences is being a member and for two years president of an ecumenical group of clergy wives. The group meet in turn in each other's homes, with each hostess deciding the format of the meeting. There is regular Bible study and an opportunity to compare events in the Bible with what is happening in their own lives. 'This has helped to create a good feeling among the denominations. We can understand that there are the same problems as well as the same joys being experienced by all of us and we can give one another support because there is a lot of sharing and mutual trust,' she says.

With such a variety of roles and such an opportunity for travel, Olga is well placed to reflect upon some of the troubles experienced by the people of the diocese. She says that there is a sense of isolation felt by many people due to the scattered nature of the islands. The region suffers from a number of natural disasters including hurricanes, earthquakes and even volcanic eruptions.

In the last three years, Hurricanes Luis and Marilyn have devastated a number of islands, including Antigua, St Kitts and Montserrat, causing severe dislocation of families. For the past year and a half, the people of Montserrat have been suffering from the continuous effects of an erupting volcano. The capital, Plymouth, is now a ghost town as residents have been evacuated to 'safe havens' in the north of the island. Many of the shelters are inadequate for the number of homeless people they have to cater for. As they try to cope, families have been broken up through migration to England and neighbouring Caribbean islands.

Olga says, 'As a result of these natural disasters, there have been many opportunities to show love and care for people in distress. Churches throughout the diocese mobilise supplies of food, clothing, toilet articles, baby food for victims of the disasters. Young people's groups and service organisations are all engaged in fund-raising activities. Church women in the diocese have been involved in the collection and distribution of relief supplies for hurricane and volcano victims and in arranging brief visits of groups of children and the elderly out of Montserrat. The Church is also involved in assessing the psychological trauma caused by these disasters and providing counselling in cases of need.'

Olga's prayer

Most loving and merciful Saviour, we thank you for calling us to work with you in this part of your vineyard. Grant that what we have done is to your honour and glory and for the good of your people here. May we ever know the joy of serving you through service to our fellow men, through Jesus Christ our Lord,

Amen

Shamim Malik – Pakistan

Fact file

Name: Shamim Malik
Date of birth: 18 October 1951
Husband: Alexander John Malik, Bishop of Lahore,
 Pakistan
Children: Three daughters, Nudrat, Nadia, Sarah; one
 son, Shaleem
First language: Punjabi

We have not visited Pakistan since my husband has been
archbishop, but I had a wonderful three weeks there in
1985 with a friend. We were visiting Andrew, my younger
son, who was having a 'gap' year before going to university.
He was at a Christian technical college in Gujranwala, near
Lahore, teaching English to the students. It was a very good
experience for him and I fell in love with the country.

It was my first visit to South East Asia and I was fascinated
by the culture. It was so totally different from Europe and
North America, which were then the only continents I had
visited. It was exciting to be in the midst of a cacophony of
sound. Everybody seemed to keep their finger on the horn of
their vehicle whether it was a car, bus, lorry, taxi or bicycle.
The animals being herded along or pulling wagons added
their noise, and then there were street vendors everywhere
selling colourful wares and intriguing food. The place was

teeming with people; many of them were just sitting around, others were wandering aimlessly and a few seemed to be bustling about their business. New smells assaulted my nose, mainly fragrant and pleasing, and the whole vista was a mass of colour. I tingled with excitement at the thought of the three weeks ahead of me.

Since that visit my fascination with the country has remained and I am delighted to be able to highlight it for you and introduce my next contributor, Shamim Malik.

The Islamic Republic of Pakistan came into being in 1947. Before that it had been part of the huge country of India. It has a very turbulent political history, including the secession of its eastern region, established as Bangladesh in 1971.

Pakistan is bordered on the west by Iran, on the north by Afghanistan and by China on the north-east. India covers the whole of the east and south-east border and the Arabian Sea is to the south.

The family organisation is strongly patriarchal with large extended family units. The social status of women in this culture is particularly low and I experienced something of this in my short time there. However, from the urban middle-income group have come many leading women politicians, journalists and teachers, who are beginning to bring about change, and many more girls are now having a good education.

Urdu is the first national language. In spite of efforts at one time to remove English, it has been recognised as indispensable and therefore is an official language. Almost the entire population is Muslim, with Hindus and Christians only a tiny percentage.

The United Church of Pakistan was a denomination inaugurated in Pakistan in 1970 consisting of former Anglican, Methodist, Scottish Presbyterian, Lutheran and mission bodies. It was the first Church in the world to join

Lutheran with Anglican, Methodist and Presbyterian and one of three to which Anglican and Methodist united, the other two being the Churches of North and South India. The Church is very active towards the poor and has initiated many development projects and provides many teachers, social workers and medical personnel.

The United Church of Pakistan became a full member of the Anglican Communion following the recommendation of the 1988 Lambeth Conference. For a minority Church in a country it is very important that they have the support of a world-wide family and can rely on them for prayer and practical help.

I am glad they are such a significant part of this Anglican family and so pleased to have Shamim telling her story.

Shamim Malik

'My father was a convert from the Muslim faith. I can still see him, his face radiant, singing choruses and psalms,' Shamim says fondly of the man who was more than a father, who became a spiritual role model. Her mother died when she was ten years old, leaving her father to bring up the family of six, five of them sons. He himself had lost his mother at a very young age and had suffered much at the hands of his stepmother. He never married again.

'My mother's ailment had drained my father both emotionally and financially. There was no support from our relatives. Nevertheless, my father remained firm in his belief and never once broke down under the criticism of his family and friends. My childhood evenings were spent listening to Bible stories and the miracles of Jesus, and this is where I got my Christian faith from. Had I not witnessed my father's strength and faith, Christianity

113

would not have been such an important part of my life,' she says proudly.

As a teenager, her days were spent either in school or in the kitchen, acting as 'mother' to her brothers. Her life was full of responsibilities and she remembers being deprived of the frivolities that her contemporaries enjoyed. 'I learnt the harsh realities of life at a young age and my practical life began when I was only a teenager. Yet I enjoyed every moment and never felt the burden that my classmates claimed I should be feeling. I was satisfied with what I had, but the absence of a mother and a sister left a vacuum that still sometimes nudges at me.'

Shamim greets the question, 'How did you meet your husband?' with a thoughtful, interested response. In the West, she guesses, such a question is probably as significant to the individual as one's basic education. 'In my part of the world the choice of a life partner is a carefully calculated task in which all the elders of the family partake. Once the family elders have given their consent, the boy who is to be married is consulted. In the case of a girl, she may or may not have a say in her parents' choice of her life partner. Such "arranged marriages" are very common in my part of the world.'

The arrangements for her own marriage were the same as these, except for the fact that she and Malik had met before and talked on several occasions before their engagement. In another departure from the norm, the family elders allowed the couple to meet and write to each other after their engagement. Malik left for Canada a week after this ceremony and they wrote to each other regularly during this time of study. They were married two years later in February 1973, when Shamim was twenty-two years of age.

Shamim discovered very early on that being a pastor's wife meant that it was almost impossible for her to pursue a career. Malik started a primary school in his parish, and due to lack of financial backing Shamim found herself working as a teacher. 'Soon, I realised that to run a school and a pastor's home simultaneously was next to impossible. I was needed at both places at the same time, especially at home to entertain guests. Being a pastor's wife was a full-time job in itself, and after a year of teaching I left the school.'

She illustrates the dedication and full-time nature of her role with a story: 'On a winter's night a young American phoned us from some club. We were not familiar with the man and did not know how he had come across our phone number. The young man insisted that if the pastor did not see him immediately, he would commit suicide. As we had had no such experiences before, my husband and I became very worried. It was very late in the night and the club was a long distance away. Malik prayed and left. I still remember the hours of restlessness and tension as I awaited my husband's return. When he finally got back, he told me that the young man was drunk and needed someone to relate his problems to. After listening to this foreigner's story, my husband took him back to his wife and counselled them both to help solve their differences.'

From the beginning of their ministry together, Shamim has held the view that the Church is a family where each one has a different yet significant role. Although she has never held a job marked with a monthly salary, she knows that she works more hours than most people. She has focused her ministry towards the women of the Church.

'In a society where women are neither aware of their rights nor are they granted any, my work was cut out for me,' she admits. 'I began from our parish at Christ Church and then slowly extended and reached out to the rural areas. When I began, I was twenty-one years of age and there were many other women in the parish of the same age. We began a youth group, held Bible studies, went out for picnics with other youth groups. Many a time I had to plead with a young girl's parents to let her join in the church's activities. Gradually, we began summer camps and I felt that the participating women were becoming aware of their rights and felt confident to voice them. It was a time of learning for me as well.

'Today, my experience with women of all age groups has become the most important part of my service in the Church,' she declares. Nowadays, as a bishop's wife she works with bigger groups including the Young Women's Christian Association and Women's Fellowship at a number of different churches. She also works with the Technical Services Association which provides education for the under-privileged women of Pakistani society. It teaches them how to provide for themselves and for their families, with instruction in basic skills like sewing, stitching, embroidery and other domestic jobs. But the women are also given 'leadership training' and attend weekly seminars on issues concerning women in Pakistan.

One of the frustrations of such a busy life is that Shamim finds she is unable to devote herself completely to either her work or her family. There has always been a conflict between the two. She strongly feels that her private life, and perhaps her children, have suffered due to the constant attention that their ministry together requires. 'When my children were younger, frequently I had to forgo their bathing and feeding time to attend to someone who needed help or a few moments of my time. Our summer vacations were almost always spent doing our routine work as both of us could not leave the office at the same time. As my involvement in the Church grew the situation worsened.'

She remembers the trauma of this was felt most sharply at the time of the birth of their youngest daughter, Sarah. She had been in labour for eighteen hours when the doctor decided to operate. He required her husband's permission to perform the operation, but Malik was in a very important meeting. 'As best I could, I convinced the doctor to carry out the operation without my husband's permission even if it was against the hospital regulations. The operation was successful, but from the above incident you can imagine the almost unreasonable demands and pressures on our time.'

Malik became a bishop at the surprisingly young age of thirty-six, when their eldest daughter Nudrat was only seven. It was a time when the children needed the attention of both parents, and Shamim says honestly that Malik had very little time to spend with his family. As a result she found herself having to attend parent–teacher meetings and other such important events alone.

Nevertheless, she threw herself into her husband's new role, accompanying him on many parish tours. This itself was a conflict, because the people of the parishes expected her to be with him, overlooking the fact that a young family needed looking after. But she found that people also thought that, being a bishop's wife, she had an authority which she plainly felt she didn't have. She explained to them that only her husband had authority.

With the women, she found it could be different. They looked up to her as a role model. 'Their aspirations, work, changing patterns of life and other such issues demanded my guidance. For the past twenty-two years, as a minister's wife, I have helped oppressed women, those who are victims of circumstances, deprived of their rights and mistreated at the hands of society. I have also worked with orphans and handicapped children.

'Sometimes,' she confesses, 'the only help I can offer is a few moments of my time and a few words of consolation to give them strength and guide them through the crisis in their lives.'

Prayer has always been a major part of Shamim's life and she describes how through the experience of prayer Christ has become a greater and greater reality. 'To me He is more than just a historic figure. He has become the true 'saviour', guiding me in my service to the Church and helping me to learn with an open heart.' She and Malik pray together twice a day, first in the early morning. A family time in the late evening is not only for prayer but for fellowship, where they all talk about the events of the day. Besides praying with the family, Shamim has a small prayer group every Saturday. Each day there are three levels of prayer: prayers for the family, prayers for diocesan workers and prayers for the universal Church.

Shamim's prayer

Please pray for the bishop of the diocese of Lahore; for his co-workers in this ministry; for his children that they may be true ambassadors of Christ wherever they go and wherever they work. Pray that people who work in this diocese should take their work as a commitment to Christ not just a means of their earning, especially in a country where the majority of people are not Christian.

Amen

Thelma Mehaffey – Northern Ireland

Fact file

Name: Thelma Mehaffey
Date of birth: 19 May 1932
Husband: James Mehaffey, Bishop of Derry and Raphoe,
Northern Ireland
Children: Philip, who died in 1993 aged 35; Wendy,
married to Andy, with twin girls; Timothy, married to
Julia, with one son

Northern Ireland is hardly ever out of the news. Peace has
eluded this beautiful country for too long. Generations have
known nothing but conflict. Thelma's sharing of her story
with us will help us to understand what the troubles are
about and how the conflict has affected their lives and
those they minister to.

I have met Thelma several times, at Mothers' Union
functions in London and when we paid an official visit
to the churches of Northern Ireland and the Republic of
Ireland in November 1994. We had the privilege of being
their guests in the diocese of Derry and Raphoe and stayed
a night in their home.

Londonderry is the second largest city in Northern Ireland
with a population of 90,000. Its roots lie in the founding of
a monastery by St Columba in the sixth century. It is a
walled city; the walls, measuring one mile in circumference

and pierced by four gates, are in a remarkable state of preservation.

Derry has become a regenerated city with a vibrant artistic and cultural life which is shared by both sides of the community. We were able to spend time in schools where we saw projects that were teaching children how to mediate and resolve conflict. On a walking tour we saw not just the history and beauty of the city but how the Inner City Trust, established in 1980, has the dual purpose of creating jobs and regenerating the Walled City. About four hundred and fifty people have already been placed in either training or employment. The churches of all denominations are involved in these projects.

The first IRA ceasefire was very new when we were there and there was an aura of disbelief that it had come about. The conflict had been going on for so long that the optimism was cautious. People on both sides desperately wanted it to work. We have seen since then the fragility of the peace process after the first ceasefire broke down. At the time of writing there are increasing signs of hope after a second ceasefire was declared by the IRA.

I am grateful to Thelma for sharing her story. It will help us to understand the situation and be able to pray all the more intelligently for it.

Thelma Mehaffey

Thelma was born and brought up in Londonderry although neither of her parents were from the area. Her mother, a nurse, was from Glasgow, and met her father, from Galway, when she was on holiday near Londonderry. Thelma had only one sister, who was eleven years younger, and feels that to all intents and purposes she was brought up as an only child.

'Growing up, I had Roman Catholic friends and our neighbours were Roman Catholics. My parents' background also meant there was no built-in prejudice against Catholics and I believe this was a helpful asset in my upbringing.'

Thelma was brought up in the Presbyterian Church as a result of her mother's strong commitment to the Church of Scotland. Her father was nominally Church of Ireland. 'Going to church and Sunday School every week was a feature of my life due to my mother's influence. As a child I spent a lot of time in Scotland and also went to school there for a time when my grandmother was ill.' To this day her mother, aged ninety-one, still refers to Scotland as home.

She remembers a happy childhood and teenage years, enjoying school and excelling enough to be awarded a university scholarship. She belonged to the Londonderry Girl Crusaders' class and eventually became an assistant leader, a position she gave up only when she was married. 'Going to Easter and summer camps was a highlight for me and I met many friends then from different parts of Ireland. Over forty years later I am still in touch with some of them,' she says.

At the age of seventeen she went to Magee University College in Londonderry. She did two years and one term there before going to Trinity College, Dublin, to finish the four-year course. Magee was a small college where the majority of students were men preparing for ministry in the Presbyterian Church. In contrast Dublin was a big change, and Thelma found it difficult. 'There were large numbers at lectures, in comparison to Magee where I was the only student in my year doing German and hence had a lecturer all to myself while I was there.'

Yet she soon got used to the change, through retaining

her links with Crusaders and joining the Evangelical Union, and became very happy. It was at Trinity she met James, who was one year senior to her. But it was only during her last term that their friendship developed. 'We both belonged to the Evangelical Union so we probably had been together in a group without really being aware of each other. In fact, I have a photograph of four of us taken at an EU party and my husband is in it even though we were not going out together then.'

One of her friends was from the same home town as James and he asked her to introduce Thelma to him. 'I still remember the three of us chatting outside the reading room in Trinity College. Later one of his friends arranged a foursome to play croquet at his home, and from then on we did quite a few things together as a foursome.' That friend was later to be best man at their wedding.

The fact that she knew James was going to be a clergyman before they married made it easier to accept the role of priest's wife. 'I fell in love with the person Jim Mehaffey and saw no problem with the fact that he was going to be ordained,' she says.

Nevertheless, moving house and parish has been a problem. Thelma easily puts down roots and then finds it difficult to leave. Yet she realises that in spite of her inner resistance each move has placed her in a happier position than before. 'Home for me is wherever we are living at the present moment. Moving means working at putting a home together again, and for a wife it is a busy time. Your husband is also very busy, but outside the home, and you have to cope with the humdrum affairs of the house.'

She enjoys being told, 'You don't look like a bishop's wife!' She retorts, 'What are we supposed to look like?' While she finds great privileges in the life, like opportunities to meet important people, to visit interesting places and to have a greater share in his ministry, nevertheless there is the other side.

'I suppose there is a certain loneliness in being the wife of a clergyman. I have always tried to treat all parishioners and wives of clergy in the same way and not become over friendly with anyone. My close friends are neither parishioners nor clergy wives,' she says.

When they married in 1956 Thelma gave up her teaching. She remembers that at the time this did not seem to be so much of a problem as it is for many clergy wives now. Most women did not continue work following marriage, she explains. She did not even contemplate returning full time to teaching when the family was growing up, although she did teach adults German one night per week for a short time.

After James had served as curate in Belfast and London and then completed four years as rector of Kilkeel in County Down, they moved back to Belfast in 1966. Their youngest child went to school, and after nine years of always having a child at home she found she was on her own again. This was a lonely period in her life, and it helped to be offered a job in a nearby school on a part-time/temporary basis. As with so many jobs of this type, it became full time and permanent and she completed thirteen years there, eventually becoming head of the English department. 'Because it was so near to the rectory I was able to be home before the children, and this was important to me.'

After fourteen years as rector of St Finnian's, Belfast, James was elected Bishop of Derry and Raphoe in 1980. Thelma gave up her teaching job and found herself developing a new role as a bishop's wife. Whenever she speaks to the wives of curates or ordinands she always says that a wife's first duty is to love and support her husband. 'If teaching in Sunday School, singing in the choir, leading women's groups, makes her unhappy she should not do it. This is not helping her husband. A home needs to be a place where renewal is found,' she declares, 'and if a wife is unhappy because she is doing things she does not enjoy, home is not then a place of renewal.'

Her main involvement since 1980 has been with the Mothers' Union at branch, diocesan and national level. She is now All-Ireland President of the Mothers' Union. This role gives her networks which James does not always have access to, and so together they can build up a picture of the parishes. It is a great privilege to be the All-Ireland President and Thelma is enjoying it immensely.

As far as possible she tries to accompany her husband to everything at which she would be welcome. Unlike their English counterparts Irish bishops do not have a chauffeur, so she shares the driving, especially on long journeys such as to Dublin, where the central committees of the Church meet.

Another emphasis which she has brought to the role is having an open home. Gatherings of clergy wives, retired clergy, widows, the chapters of the two cathedrals, Mothers' Union members and so on are all welcome. 'The difference between being a rector's wife and the bishop's wife,' she jokes, 'is that the numbers are much larger. I had to acquire extra plates at an early stage in our life in Londonderry.'

Thelma is also the timekeeper for James's sermons, always informing him if they are too long or too short. She finds herself being a sounding board for ideas and a confidential listener.

'In Northern Ireland we live in a divided society. There is segregation in housing and in education. A lot of young people grow up not knowing anyone of a different Christian tradition. A lot has been done to remedy this situation but a lot remains to be done.'

She identifies sectarianism as the major problem of society in Northern Ireland. 'We live in a violent society. Over thirty of our parishioners have been murdered by the paramilitary since my husband became bishop in 1980. A lot of them had close links with the Church. I can think of one churchwarden who was shot in front of his wife and two children. We are reminded of these killings when we go to the parishes where they worshipped and see the memorial tablets on the wall,' Thelma says sadly.

Nevertheless, there is a great respect for the Church of Ireland as a moderate Church which is prepared to talk to all sides. They live in Londonderry where the majority are Roman Catholics. When in 1982 one of the parish churches lost its roof in a violent storm the first fund-raising event was organised by the local Roman Catholic church.

Thelma and James find lots of opportunities to counteract sectarianism by building better community relations. The main churches work closely together on a whole range of issues. In the past they have taken both Roman Catholic and Protestant teenagers to the United States so that they could get to know each other. This, she remembers, exploded loads of myths: 'I didn't know you Protestants believed in the Virgin Mary!' She declares: 'We try to reach out to those who do not belong to our Church. This can be done without giving up our commitment to our own Church.'

Thelma and James lost their son Philip in 1993, when he was thirty-five years old. It was his courageous attitude to his own death, as the result of a terminal illness, which sustained them. 'Without being morbid he was able to talk about his death and funeral and that was a great help to us,' she remembers. 'He was also keen for his father to speak at the funeral. The fact that he lived in Germany made it harder for us as we could not be with him all the time. We are so proud of the way Philip approached his death. When he realised his illness was terminal we made a conscious decision to make the most of whatever time was left. So time together or talking on the phone were highlights for us all.

'The prime thing that sustained us was our belief in the resurrection. I do not know how people who have no Christian belief cope with personal loss. At a time of crisis one clings on to one's faith. There is healing and with the passage of time the happy memories outweigh the sad ones,' she says. 'Having had the experience of losing a son we are better equipped to help people in similar situations.'

Renewal through difficult times comes from walking on the deserted beaches of Donegal with her husband. 'The beauty of the place is constant, whether the sun shines or the rain is beating down. After Philip's death the healing began when we spent some days in County Donegal.'

Thelma's prayer

(*A prayer written especially for the diocese of Derry and Raphoe and used in the diocese for the Decade of Evangelism.*)

Almighty God, give us an enduring vision of your purpose for your Church in this diocese. Help us to become what you would make us and to walk in the path which you set before us. Grant joy in success and patience in adversity. Renew us in faith, in hope and in love, that we may be enabled to reach out and to serve the communities in which we live. We offer our prayer through Him in whose resurrection we have life and in whose pattern we would live, your Son, our Saviour, Jesus Christ.

Amen

Irene Mhogolo – Tanzania

Fact file

Name: Irene Mhogolo
Date of birth: 14 June 1948
Husband: Godfrey Mdimi Mhogolo, Bishop of the
  diocese of Central Tanganyika, Tanzania
Children: Two sons, Nyemo and Wendo; one daughter,
  Lisa

We had a wonderful official visit to Tanzania in 1993.
We visited several dioceses and the diocese of Central
Tanganyika was one of them. There was a wonderful service
in Dodoma in the cathedral compound to celebrate the very
new, nearly completed bell tower of the cathedral, which still
has to be built. Mdimi orchestrated that service which was
full of marvellous indigenous music and dancing and also
of the very traditional. Indeed we heard the 'Hallelujah
Chorus' sung beautifully by one of the local choirs.

The service was out in the open with very little protection
from the blazing sun, and it lasted for many hours. At the
end, many wonderful gifts were given to us by different
groups in the diocese. My lasting memory of the occasion
was of a Mothers' Union group dancing towards us in their
colourful national costume followed by HM Ambassador,
Roger Westbrook. On returning from ascertaining that his
driver had some water to drink, he got caught up in the

procession and joined in, in the spirit of the occasion, by dancing with the Mothers' Union back to his front seat. He received a round of applause and took his bow. Quite uncharacteristic of a British diplomat, but this particular man had endeared himself to the Tanzanians, showing tremendous interest and helping them with many projects during his time in their country.

We were privileged to visit the home of Mdimi and Irene and meet their three wonderful children. They were full of fun and not at all subdued by the visit of an archbishop as long as he would play with them! That made it very special and memorable for us.

I am so pleased that Irene has been willing to contribute to this book. That has not been without its difficulties: her first manuscript of answers to the questionnaire went astray in the post and because of the lack of office equipment she did not have a copy of it. She offered to do it again so I sent out another questionnaire. When it was completed, Irene managed to get someone travelling to England to post it on their arrival. Thankfully that worked, and we have a moving account of Irene's life.

Irene Mhogolo

At the age of twenty-four Irene was a young Australian nurse working in London, setting out through the fog and the street lights at 7 a.m. each day, and going back home at 8 p.m. through the fog and the street lights again.

'It wasn't an ideal existence for someone who loves sunshine, so when a friend mentioned a two-month visit to Tanzania to see friends, I was more than ready to go with her.' Thus a train of events were set in motion that eventually led to the unlikely conclusion of this Australian girl becoming the wife of a Tanzanian bishop.

Irene and Mdimi met at the Mvumi Hospital in the diocese of Central Tanganyika, famous world-wide as the 'Jungle Doctor' hospital. She takes up the story: 'We stayed overnight, and in the evening were with a group of hospital staff and some visitors on a New Life for All safari in the area. I was introduced by an English lady missionary to a young Tanzanian pastor on the New Life team and he told me he was soon going to Australia to study.'

He suggested that they might see each other there, with a typical non-Australian's lack of grasp of the awesome size of this land mass. Her home was a thousand miles from Melbourne, the city in which he was to stay. But her scepticism was unjustified. Four years later they found themselves studying in adjoining colleges in Melbourne.

Irene's father was a priest, ordained just before World War II. Her parents married shortly after the war ended, when he came home from service in Papua New Guinea. The earliest memory she has is of a parish council meeting in her home, and as a little girl watching in fascination as one lady knitted furiously throughout the meeting.

When she was four years old the family, with Irene and her brother, moved to a lovely farming area. The community was small and everyone knew everything about each other. 'Life revolved around the church, Country Women's Association, the Red Cross and the Returned Servicemen's Club. As a family, our life was the church; constrained at times because my father had become chronically ill. He died when I was twelve and had just finished primary schooling.'

So the family were uprooted from the countryside to suburbia. Irene can recall being aware of God's existence and of His love for the family and the community, through all the good times and also the trauma of her father's death. She and her brother absorbed and came to know by heart the words of the services in the Book of Common Prayer, many of the psalms and most of the Gospels. Sunday School helped to lay the foundation of gospel truths and songs which reinforced them. Later youth groups, she found, were boring and insipid in comparison.

She trained as a nurse and then, in her mid-twenties, became part of a strong hospital Bible study group which, she says, 'brought me face to face with what I believed, and why, and catapulted me out of a comfortable and secure job in Australia to a remote village in Northern Ethiopia'. This, she says, is when her faith grew and her spiritual adventures began.

The greatest adventure was to be her marriage to Mdimi and move to Tanzania – a country listed by the World Bank as the second poorest in the world. At first, Irene had to be realistic about the 'cross-cultural' nature of the marriage. 'Was I prepared for the consequences? How would our families react? But it would also be a marriage to a pastor, about which I'd already had some insight in my own family and during my stay of eventually thirteen months in Tanzania. Our life would not only revolve around the church, but be severely controlled by its demands. And in a different culture, what then? Could I curb my natural "Western" responses, objections or preferences and put my husband's call and responsibilities in first place? I thought I could.'

In fact some of her fears were unfounded. Both families reacted with love and encouragement. She found the Tanzanian Church to be supportive, while 'Western' church communities were surprisingly far less enthusiastic. 'This provided me with an insight into the racial prejudice lying so close to the surface in so many human beings, and became another period of growth for my own faith.'

Even when Irene and Mdimi had made their decision to get married, the final arbiter was his bishop. 'I was working six thousand miles away from both my own home and my future husband, and the local postal service was often erratic. I received one letter from Mdimi telling me that the bishop had been informed of our plans and asked to approve them, and that he had asked for one month to pray about his decision.

'The next day there was no mail at all, and none for the next few weeks. That meant I was given a special time to pray and to consider, all over again, what my choices and responses would be. If the bishop said "yes", was I really prepared to accept all that was involved? If the answer was "no", what would I do? Collapse in tears and go home? Or continue to work in yet another culture with its mixture of blessings and headaches, and do it with a smile?'

After five weeks she eventually found peace of mind and heart. She decided that she would be able to live with the demands of a 'yes' and the disappointment of a 'no'. The very next day the mail 'drought' was broken. The sackful included a telegram with a very simple message: 'Bishop approves us'.

'Living in another culture is always a learning process. Being a pastor's wife in another culture is a baptism of fire. As a pastor here my husband is greatly respected, and a great many demands are made on his time by other people. These people frequently have priority. I've had to spend a lot of my time in the last fifteen years learning to be patient, learning to discern real and imagined demands by other people and trying to compensate my children for the time they don't have with their father,' she says.

Mdimi occasionally travels overseas but most frequently within his diocese. Although geographically Central Tanganyika is one of the smaller dioceses in the province it is one of the largest in terms of Anglican Christians, with two hundred and fifty thousand in 165 parishes. The custom is to hold confirmation services in each parish each year, which can only be done during the dry season from May to December. This means frequent trips away, for three to ten nights at a time with only one or two nights in between each trip to read the mail and have his clothes laundered.

'In this culture, the bishop and his wife are seen to be father and mother to the diocese and expected to fill these roles literally,' she explains. 'Mdimi enjoys these trips as pastoral visits, and so do I whenever I can go too. However, many people expect me to accompany him all the time, and are quick to voice their inability to understand why I do not, despite knowing that we have three children at school. I find their constant comments very difficult at times.'

Back at home, she finds a great number of people come to her with problems and requests. Some, she says, genuinely need her action or advice. Some can be referred to other diocesan personnel, but all take time. 'Our culture requires that each person sit down, be greeted and be heard, at whatever length. The favourite visiting time is in the early evening – not the easiest time of day to juggle visitors, cooking and children,' she says.

Irene's life has been dominated by choices, and she finds that throughout her ministry and that of Mdimi these have continued unabated. In nursing, she says, the choices were what to do next and where to do it. In each situation she found herself praying that she would know clearly what to do, after looking at all the factors involved.

'The choices in my ministry continue, and are very varied, but usually consist of deciding what to do first, which areas have priority, and when (or if) to say "no". The last one is by far the most difficult,' she admits. Her work with women and girls in the diocese, she knows, will affect her own children in some way. One of the most demanding roles is as diocesan president of the Mothers' Union. This is an automatic job for the bishop's wife. She says she has managed to cope with this role with lots of forward planning and help from a few friends and neighbours.

'Our children have their needs and wants, and I try to make them a priority when it seems reasonable. They enjoy an English-language Sunday School, a youth group and Brownies weekly and need supervision with homework and music each afternoon. I'm their "transport officer" for these school activities.

'Many of the tensions involved have their origins in local culture, and in the Church as a subculture. Our lifestyle has changed enormously to try and accommodate both, but this does not always "accommodate" the growth or the needs of a Christian family,' she says.

She has a love for Tanzania and its people after all her years there. The main problems of the country are an enormous lack of education, health care and investment capital. Tanzania is also afflicted by a large unemployment problem. Women face the additional problem of having little access to work and not being helped by any legal framework.

'AIDS', she says, 'is devastating the country, particularly affecting educated men and younger women (who are the farmers). Alcohol abuse also is increasing among women.' Yet despite this daunting list of problems, Irene is convinced that opportunities exist within the Church itself as there is complete freedom to preach the gospel and to teach in the villages and towns.

The Church takes seminars to villages with topics varying from Christian growth to Christian marriage, AIDS, traditional practices affecting the health of women and children, stewardship, leadership and the roles of women and children in the Church.

Irene says, 'Prayer has become more and more important over the years, as finding time to pray alone or for any length of time becomes more difficult. Prayer now more often takes the form of "Please let me do this the right way". But there are longer times, too, of praise and thanks for answered prayer and for peace of mind when the choices have had to be made in some haste or have been especially difficult.'

Irene's prayer

Father God, thank you for your love for Mdimi and Irene and their children. Give them physical and mental strength in all they do for you day by day. Give them wisdom, patience and good health, and as you are blessing them, allow them to be a blessing to others, for Jesus' sake.

Amen

Eleci Neves – Brazil

Fact file

Name: Eleci Passos Pereira Neves
Date of birth: 24 April 1943
Husband: D. Jubal Pereira Neves, Diocesan Bishop of
 South-western Brazil
Children: None
First language: Portuguese

Sadly, in all our visits through the Anglican Communion
George and I have not travelled on the great continent of
South America. That is a treat we have still to come and I
know it will be very exciting.

I met Eleci very briefly at the end of April 1997, and
look forward to getting to know her better at the Lambeth
Conference in the summer of 1998. However, I met Jubal
for longer, in the USA in September 1995, when there was
a conference on evangelism, bringing together people from
many countries of the Anglican Communion to share their
experiences of the Decade of Evangelism in their country.
The contribution was outstanding from Brazil, and Eleci
describes in this chapter the burning passion of Brazilian
Anglicans to share their faith with the needy and all
they encounter.

Brazil, like most developing nations, has a young population. Just under half are below the age of twenty, but

with the modernisation of society there is an increase in life expectancy and a lowering of the birth rate, along with a general lowering of the population growth rate. Despite such changes the infant mortality rate has remained high, although as would be expected it varies considerably between the affluent urban districts and the poorer country communities.

The Episcopal (Anglican) Church of Brazil owes its roots to the work of American missionaries who went over to start the Church. There were other small parallel groups who went to serve the English-speaking and the Japanese-speaking communities. These communities have dwindled and their descendants have naturally become Brazilian, so the ministry now is to Portuguese-speaking congregations. However, provision continues for those who want their own language, and, to quote from diocesan information, 'after all the very presence of these facilities was, under God, their gift'.

Almost 90 per cent of the Brazilian people are Roman Catholics, making it the largest country of that faith in the world. Among the other religions, the majority are Protestants dominated increasingly by fundamentalist and Pentecostal sects.

These facts make the story in this chapter all the more surprising and I am delighted that Eleci has told it, in spite of the trouble she had to go to in getting it translated from her native Portuguese to English, to share it with us.

Eleci Neves

In the tradition that has marked the contribution of the mainstream Churches at their best in South America, Eleci Neves has, like her husband Jubal, always had a ministry with the 'unprotected, the most fragile and with social justice to the destitute and abandoned, old and young'.

'This is a ministry,' she says, 'which is often not appreciated by the parish communities. Only a small group of people dedicate themselves to living faith outside the Church, searching to obey Christ in what He announced and was sent to do: help the weak, the oppressed, the sick, the leper, those who suffer injustice.'

It was the changing circumstances and all the moving which Jubal has needed to do in his ministries which led Eleci out of her career in accountancy and banking to get more involved in the social service of the Church.

She describes Brazil as a country of serious socio-economic instability and 'maladjustment in the family'. She deplores the influence of the media, and especially soap operas, which give people the idea of personal and family happiness based on material possessions. 'This imported, free and unattached family life is no good for any family in any part of the world,' she says. 'Through soap operas, many people copy a modernism filled with attitudes of violence, individualism, triviality towards sex, with personal success as the key to happiness. It is a "dog eat dog" world,' she says.

She is especially concerned with the families of priests and with the widows, giving them attention during times of depression, when they move town or are bereaved. 'We in the diocese have been working for some time with "Encounters" of couples, women, youth and children, creating opportunities to celebrate "tenderness amid the conflicts", and also encouraging and facilitating models and values for their lives as Christians.

'At the moment we are looking at how we can help singles who need something from the Church in terms of participation in the fellowship of the Christian community and giving them an emotional balance where their self-esteem can grow, through solidarity, service and through spirituality.'

The Bishop and I

Eleci was born in a town called Jaguarao, in the state of Rio Grande do Sul, on the border of Brazil and Uruguay. The River Jaguarao formed the division between the two countries. Her parents, Carlos and Wanda, had a cattle farm. 'My childhood and adolescence were very healthy because of the almost daily presence of friends, cousins, uncles, aunts and grandparents. I am convinced today that those hours talking with my grandparents and godparents, about life experiences that they shared with me through their stories, were something that affected me a lot in terms of behaviour and way of life.'

She remembers her parents' relationship fondly. Her father was twelve years older than her mother, and she says, 'At that time men believed that they always had to have the last word. They were also different in the way they were, but the good thing about their life as a couple is that they complemented each other well so as to give their children a good life education. In her affectionate and gentle way, my mother managed to persuade him even when it involved outings and entertainment for the children.'

All of the family were Roman Catholic and Eleci's primary education was in a Catholic school. She became a Daughter of Mary and remembers how, on every Friday and Sunday during May, the Daughters took part in the Mass dressed in white, and threw white and red rose petals on the image of Mary.

Her adolescence was filled with regular visits to the cinema, balls and many sports, such as volleyball, handball and running. On the farm they went horse-riding, had picnics and went swimming in streams. On some occasions they would ride out to collect ostrich and chicken eggs, which they found on the ground, for food. 'Another beautiful thing, I remember, my mother used to do especially with me, was to observe the wild flowers, the sunrise, the dusk falling and the stars in the sky.' As a result, Eleci came to love creation, and now regards it as much a place of worship as anywhere else. She finds that being in the countryside helps her carry out her devotion and prayers.

As an older teenager she and some friends were invited to a benefit ball at school. 'After they insisted a lot I decided to go. The women were on one table and the men on another. Among the men, there was the son of the parish priest of the local Anglican church, and also Jubal. The two of them came over and asked us to dance. I had already heard about him through my sister who told me about the new priest who had arrived in town.' She recalls a strange gesture from Jubal: when the ribbon on her shoe came undone, he picked it up and put it in his jacket pocket. The next day her friends invited her to an outing into the countryside with the youth of the Anglican church. After a day of games it became evident that Jubal was taking an interest in the young Eleci. He started to wait for her outside the bank where she worked.

Yet their courtship was not without opposition. A Roman Catholic nun commented in a visit to her grandmother: 'What a pity, Dona Gustavina, that your granddaughter Eleci is going out with a reverend from the Church of the Devil.'

Eleci explains, 'This is how many people thought of the Protestant Churches of the fifties and sixties. The Anglican Church was called Protestant and therefore was the Church of Satan. But my grandmother, wise and educated, simply replied to the sister that in her opinion it was the Church of Christ, following the Apostles, and for her Satan didn't exist and couldn't have his own Church.'

At the beginning of their marriage, Eleci gave up her job in the bank for Jubal's ministry. In retrospect, she describes this as the typical behaviour of a 'machista' man, worried because he did not want to create problems with his bishop, and as a result she lost a good job. 'But on the other hand, I had more time for the ministry of the Church, that is, to see and to be able to take a larger part in the anxieties, worries, anguish and hopes of Jubal and others in their Christian life, and I also felt a growth in my faith,' she recalls.

One painful experience for Eleci was the loss of her mother, who died suddenly without having been seriously ill. Eleci was on her own at home, a long way from her mother, and Jubal was visiting the Church in Portugal. She says, 'In my husband's ministry, at times of pain and loss of someone in the community, he is always with those who are suffering, consoling them and giving them hope. Alone, I felt very fragile, without that hug of affection from my husband and with no one to console and support me. This hard experience didn't affect our ministries, but it was a painful mark in my life.' This sad time, when Eleci had felt so clearly God's hand on her, taught her to value even more the quality time the family had together, and not to worry about the quantity, something they could do nothing about.

Eleci has been able to maintain a career as an administrator in schools, using the skills she learnt at university. She now has a micro business in computer services. This offers her the opportunity to provide material for the diocese as well as giving her the opportunity of professional achievement.

She is realistic about the conflicts on her time. 'I try to show people that in the first place I am Eleci, a lay woman who is ready to work for the Church in ways in which my vocation and gifts are best suited and in the episcopate of my husband. But the wife is always seen as a leader in everything that takes place in the Church. Jubal and I talked a lot when we thought about marriage so that he didn't expect from me a particularly active part in his work.' She says this was not her way. She strongly believes that 'the bishop's spouse, or indeed the spouse of a priest, should not have such a strong "presence" that they take up the space and participation of other lay members of the community'.

In her role as a wife of a bishop, she tries to be a motivator, 'bringing hope and dreaming together with him and the communities, so that, through work and prayer, proposals can be seen through, thus helping others and also the life of the Church'.

When she married Jubal, she remembers, her mother gave wise advice which has stayed with her always. Her mother said, 'My daughter, being the wife of the priest is a great responsibility in the community. She always has to be ready to serve and to hear people without giving any hurried advice.'

Eleci's prayer

I will worship you, Lord, with all my heart!

May the blessings of the Lord enlighten our lives so that I can serve people, and so that our Church can share spiritual growth with all.

May our words and our ways always be of hope, strengthening and encouraging.

May we, through the power of the Holy Spirit, offer people a service of love and prayer, and may the people of the South-western Brazil diocese search for a reawakening to a life of brotherly communion, in the practice of justice and tenderness.

We thank you, Lord God, for putting us in the leadership of this diocese. Strengthen our knees which are sometimes so weak, and may our missionary spirit never tire of searching for and serving others.

The Bishop and I

All this we ask, with the forgiveness of our sins, through your Son, Jesus Christ, who gave His life for us and rose again.

Amen

Maggie Nkwe – South Africa

Fact file

Name: Maggie Malethola Nkwe
Date of birth: 1 March 1938
Husband: David Cecil Tapi Nkwe, Bishop of Klerksdorp,
South Africa
Children: Kelefang Felicity Hatta, widowed in 1994, with
three children; Modike Daniel Peter; Tsipane Angela
First language: Tswana, South Sotho

I have only met Maggie, very briefly, on two occasions.
The first time was when George and I were in Cape
Town for the joint meeting of the Primates and the
Anglican Consultative Council in January 1993. We were
accommodated at the University of the Western Cape,
and towards the end of the time all the bishops and
their spouses of the Church of the province of Southern Africa came to join us for an evening. It was a
lovely celebration and each diocese shared their story
with us.

The diocese of Klerksdorp was introduced by David and
Maggie Nkwe. The diocese was created when Johannesburg
was divided into four in 1990 and it is the western 'wing'
of that formerly huge diocese. David was made the first
bishop of that newly formed diocese. It faces vast needs,
but does so with abundant prayers and often boundless

energy. 'Our aim is to build a cathedral in every heart,' says Bishop David Nkwe.

I met Maggie again in Cape Town at the end of June 1996, at another big celebration to wish Desmond and Leah Tutu a long and happy retirement. That was held at the wine estate of Vergelegen, which produces some of the finest wines of the region. It was on that occasion that Maggie handed over her completed questionnaire, which has told the story in her chapter. The following morning we were in the cathedral, both honoured to be present at a magnificent service to say farewell to two very special people who have helped to shape the new South Africa – the retiring Archbishop, Desmond, and his lovely wife, Leah.

Maggie's story is one of determination through the struggles and joys of ministry. With a great sense of fun and a very strong personality, the causes she has championed have been very fortunate to have her.

A number of the bishops' wives in South Africa felt she was the right person to contribute as a speaker at the spouses' programme of the 1998 Lambeth Conference. I am convinced she will be one of our best speakers.

Maggie Nkwe

Maggie remembers that David's first two years of ministry precipitated quite a crisis in their marriage. Like many other clergy wives, she found it difficult to come to terms with the depth of his commitment to the parish, which she believed to be at the expense of their marriage.

'I felt like I was ignored by my husband. He had to care for a parish and I think he hoped to put right all the wrongs of the parish overnight, to the detriment of his family. I prayed about my feelings and suspicions, and through God's grace I pulled myself up and came up with a programme of activities which suited me without consulting him,' she laughs.

This was a wonderful Saturday of activities, she recalls, which even included going to watch a soccer match. He was amazed to return home to find that she and her youngest child were not in the house. 'My baby and I were happy to have turned a crisis situation of brooding and feeling sorry for ourselves into a challenging day full of activities and happiness. My husband felt excluded and then gave us more attention.'

Being married to a clergyman was a rude shock. As a newly married couple neither of them knew what his calling entailed. Somehow they found they managed to take each day at a time, as they ventured into the unknown.

'My mother, Moratooq, which means "loving" and my grandmother, Angeline, are my parents who need to be mentioned in my story. My name, Malethola, means "silence", because I was born in the back room of my grandmother's workplace. Her employers did not know that we were there and I was denied my first cry, which usually gives proud parents a good feeling, lest the employer heard and my grandmother would have been in trouble.'

Maggie's father was a migrant worker who abandoned her mother and elder sister, Tselane, in Lesotho. When Maggie was born her mother was searching for him in Johannesburg. At the time she was unsuccessful in her search; later they learnt that he had married a woman from the city.

Maggie's mother was soon to remarry, this time to a divorcee. 'This was all to my detriment,' Maggie remembers. 'My stepfather did not like me, neither did I like or trust him. My salvation was my grandmother, who took me over from my mother and allowed her to adjust in her marriage.'

Maggie didn't start school until the age of ten because she had no fixed place of abode, but she worked hard and got a first-class pass in her standard six exams. Fortunately for her she became a Sunday School teacher and a choir member of her grandmother's parish, and through this the rector offered her a scholarship for high school education. As a result of this and the support of many in the parish, Maggie succeeded in going forward for her general nursing training at Baragwanath Hospital in Soweto, later studying midwifery and gaining a diploma in paediatrics.

She met David in 1956. She was in Form I and he in Form IV at Orlando High School. His story was a typical one of rural children in a search for education. His father started a school on a farm he was managing. The school only went up to a certain level, so David then had to travel to continue his education. He eventually needed to go to Johannesburg to matriculate. There he struggled to get accommodation, and eventually ended up in Maggie's township and attended the same parish church. David became a server at the church and later joined the Sunday School staff.

Maggie gives credit for their courtship to 'Aunty' Josephine Palmer, who ran the Sunday School and was a respected community leader. She used to invite the pair along to her house for tea after meetings of all the Sunday School teachers. After this they had to walk home together. 'It became inevitable for us to fall in love,' Maggie says. 'We have always tried to fight for the success of our marriage and have endeavoured to help each other in order to achieve our goal.'

This has meant that David's ministry has never been separate from their marriage commitment to each other. She has pledged herself to support him. Although she had the nursing profession and community interests she knew that, in order to make her marriage work, she was going to have to make sacrifices. Thus she has been active in the parishes and churches. But she points out that this is not merely because she is married to a priest, but comes naturally to her because of her involvement in church activities from her earliest years.

Nevertheless, Maggie's commitment to the community is demonstrated when she describes the 'second crisis' of her life in 1978. 'This was when I had to resign my lucrative post as a senior sister and pioneer primary health care nursing sister to take up a post as a director of a children's home. This home was condemned by the local authorities because of its poor physical structure and it was a home that existed on donations, a home that had no benefits.' Maggie knew that she would have to raise money for food and salaries if she took up the post. But she indicated to her husband that this was what she felt called by God to do. 'I went on to resign and sacrificed my future for the sake of abandoned infants,' she says.

With untold effort and commitment Maggie rebuilt the home over a period of years and managed to get it reregistered. When in 1990 David was made Bishop of Klerksdorp she recognised that it was time to move on. 'Because we married for better and for worse, I decided to move to Klerksdorp, 160 kilometres each way from Johannesburg. For two years I drove that distance three times a week to try and supervise the children's home. It was taxing physically, emotionally and economically. I prayed to God to provide me with someone who could take over from me. It took two years of prayer and hard work before God answered my prayers.'

Maggie now gives thanks that the home is doing so well, but she was soon to find a wealth of other opportunities in the caring field opening up to her as a bishop's wife. She is a consultant to the Mothers' Union, a founder of the Women's Desk, director of the literacy programme, co-ordinator of a youth exchange between Klerksdorp and Exeter in the United Kingdom and consultant to the pre-school programmes. Above all she goes around the diocese with her husband, meeting and getting to know the people.

'I would like to mention,' she says, 'I am not paid for the services I am offering in the poor diocese of Klerksdorp. I am a founder of the Widows' Forum, which was triggered by the death of my son-in-law in 1994. My young daughter's experience and many other widows' plights made me form a much-needed forum for widows.'

When David became bishop Maggie recalls being told by a senior bishop's wife to expect to find it the loneliest role in the world. Heeding this advice, Maggie thought it would help to accompany her husband wherever he travelled in the diocese. 'But I experienced how it is to be marginalised. The congregation always gives much attention to the bishop and they don't see the bishop's wife on arrival. It is only when he introduces his wife that she is noticed.'

She argues that a spouse has much less focus and orientation than a bishop does. 'They have synods and various activities and involvement within the Church and the secular world. A bishop's wife has no orientation, no formal or planned programmes. Hence the loneliness. Loneliness is one of the worst diseases,' she says with feeling. 'I hope something can be done to deal with the role of the bishop's wife and the need to deal with the loneliness they often suffer.'

To help her overcome this, Maggie threw herself, with the nature of an activist, into the social problems of the diocese. She cites the main problems as poverty, illiteracy and unemployment. 'I always feel helpless when I am faced with the degree and magnitude of these problems,' she says. 'I always wish we could have been sent here ten years ago when we were younger and more energetic. In travelling with my husband, I come face to face with the victims of poverty. I have also found women who feel helpless, and they seem to accept their lot as if God has destined them to suffer for the rest of their lives.'

This was why she started a Women's Desk in the Church, to help women discover their full potential and improve their self-esteem. Women's Desk seminars, she says, have produced great results. Some members have started projects such as pre-schools and literacy programmes. But funding for such projects is becoming a major problem. 'The diocese of Klerksdorp is situated in an area where the people have been marginalised and forgotten, during the apartheid regime and unfortunately even now,' she says. 'Politicians and business people often talk about the rural people without doing anything about them. I pray and hope that the Church may reach out to help us.'

Maggie's prayer

Thank you, God, for the sleep and protection. Thank you, God, for this day which I give back to you. Visit and touch my husband, David, and help him to carry out your calling in your vineyard.

Visit and touch my widowed daughter, Kelefang, with all her problems. Lord, help her visit and touch my son, Modike, and help him to find a job and realise how you care for him, Lord.

Visit and touch Tsipane, my younger daughter, and help her to pursue her career knowing that all that we have comes from you and to you should we give thanks.

Lord, make me an instrument of change for better lives in your vineyard and grant us peace.

Hail Mary, full of grace, blessed art thou amongst women

and blessed is the fruit of thy womb Jesus. Holy Mary, Mother of God, pray for us sinners, now and at the hour of our death.

Amen

Berta Sengulane – Mozambique

Fact file

Name: Esperanca Berta Zandamela Sengulane
Date of birth: 30 March 1955
Husband: Dinis Salomao Sengulane, Bishop of the
diocese of Lebombo, Mozambique
Children: Three sons, Teofilo, Crisostomo and Bruno;
one daughter, Fidelia
First language: Chopi

We visited Mozambique in June 1996, following a short
visit to Cape Town for the farewell service of Desmond
Tutu on his retirement.

On the evening of the day of our arrival in Maputo, the
capital city of Mozambique, we were invited to the home
of Dinis and Berta for an evening meal. We met their four
children, who led us in a wonderful family evensong, sung
in Portuguese. It was memorable and set us asking ourselves
how many English homes would see such a scene, of four
teenagers celebrating a service in their own home in front
of a group of strangers in such an unselfconscious way.

It was a memorable visit in so many ways, not least
because George and I celebrated our thirty-sixth wedding
anniversary on an exciting overnight trip up country for
a Eucharist attended by thousands of people. Everywhere
we went we were greeted by Christians wearing shirts or

dresses made with material printed with a picture of the Archbishop of Canterbury in wonderfully bright colours! It was a marvellous welcome indeed.

Dinis Sengulane set up an influential peace initiative by the Church, called Changing Swords into Ploughshares. We visited the Anglican Peace Centre and saw the destruction of guns which had been brought in by ordinary people in exchange for bicycles or agricultural implements or material. It also applied to children, who exchanged toy guns for toys of peace.

Dinis and Berta have been at the forefront of helping the Church to lead on peace initiatives. He has even been honoured by Her Majesty the Queen for what he has achieved.

Berta's story helps us to understand what it is like to live and bring up children in the midst of war in the country she loves. Her story has been translated into English, and I hope we have done it justice.

Berta Sengulane

Dinis and Berta married two years after Mozambique became independent in 1975. Throughout their married life they have lived in the midst of civil war. Peacemaking has been the main emphasis of their influential ministry together. Dinis has been a key negotiator for peace and eventually helped to bring an end to the fighting.

They were thrown together shortly after their government had adopted a radical Marxist doctrine and attempted to abolish the Christian faith. Berta explains: 'They closed some countryside churches and imposed restrictions such as banning baptism for young people and bringing in compulsory jobs on Sundays during the service times, which they called "voluntary work". Many people were confused, congregations were losing their members, the few people who were still attending the church found themselves neglected. This was a very dark period for the Church, with membership decreasing.'

Dinis was only a recently ordained priest. 'Inspired by the Holy Scriptures,' she says, he organised a group including Berta, another young woman and a young man to resist what they described as 'the evil that was emerging in Mozambique'.

'Our goal was the word of God,' she says. They lived especially by the biblical passage in Ezekiel 37:3–14 which says, 'Son of man, can these bones live? So I answered, O LORD God, you know. Again he said to me, prophesy to these bones, and say to them, O dry bones, hear the word of the LORD, I will put my spirit in you, and you shall live, and I will place you in your land. Then you shall know that I, the LORD, have spoken it and performed it, says the LORD.'

Berta, Dinis and their companions found that their radical Bible study was inspirational. They began to visit those Christians who, through government pressure, had ceased going to church. They told them, 'The time has come for you to turn to your Church and to be saved in Jesus Christ.'

Dinis had already been appointed Bishop of Lebombo when Berta married him in 1977. As a very young 'mother' to the diocese, Berta saw a great deal of pain and turmoil during the sixteen years of war. 'There was a lot of pain, grief, hunger and devastation. Many people were displaced and many schools, hospitals and factories were destroyed. It was a very tragic war in a way that when someone's death was announced, the tendency was to enquire about a possible attack. A natural death had become something rare,' she says sadly.

Berta believes that the experience of the war and the need to reflect on peace issues has had a deep impact on her thinking. 'Hope' is the key word she uses when thinking about her faith. She and Dinis both found great reassurance in Malachi 3:11, 'And because of you I will rebuke the devourers for your sakes, so that they will not destroy the fruit of your ground, nor shall the vine fail to bear fruit for you in the field.' With these words in mind, they began to pray before even the shortest travels from their home and they observed a thanksgiving ritual after reaching their destination.

Berta was born into a Christian family and was baptised one month after her birth. Her maternal grandfather was a catechist. She was the firstborn of nine children. Her father was a driver and her mother a housewife. 'I spent my childhood close to my parents. It was a very exciting period. I used to play with my brothers and sisters, and cousins and friends as well. Our grandparents used to tell us stories and legends, "Karingana wa Karingana". They also used to offer to each one of us various things such as cashew nuts, bananas and oranges. Above all I remember and miss their love.'

When she was nine, the family moved to a rural area called Maguluine, about twenty kilometres from their home in Maputo town, where her father could have a shop in order to increase their very low income. The move gave Berta the opportunity to attend a Roman Catholic school. She passed both the first and second standards in the same year because she was able to read fluently any book in Portuguese that was put in front of her. She remembers her childhood and teenage years as 'very blessed and joyful' times.

There was no Anglican church in Maguluine. Consequently, on Sundays the family attended Roman Catholic services. 'As I was growing up I started to persuade my young sisters to seek an Anglican church so we could be confirmed. After very hard searching we were happy to find one that was eight kilometres away. We used to walk

154

every Sunday to this church, but soon some people were kind enough to establish a new congregation at the home of my parents in 1972.' This, she says, was a way to reduce the long walks by the family, but also a church plant to serve others. Now this congregation has its own building and about two hundred members.

Being married to Dinis has affected Berta's life tremendously. She recalls: 'On the one hand, it was a great deal for me to be a bishop's wife. I saw myself as very young. I used to ask myself what I had to offer to God's people; thus I started to ask God to bless my husband's ministry and not to let me misbehave. On the other hand, to be a bishop's wife has changed my spiritual life, since I started to pray not only on Sundays,' she says. 'His ministry has positively affected my life. The status of "Mummy" or "Grandmother" that I hold in the Church as a bishop's wife has helped me to gain a spiritual maturity. The love that God's people have offered us is the best thing one can learn. I feel moved to share with others what I have heard and seen about Jesus. This is the evangelical spirit that is growing in me. My perception on peace issues has also deepened,' she explains.

Berta has worked as a clerk in the bank ever since they married. She says that she sometimes feels overloaded at weekends when she accompanies Dinis on his pastoral visits in the diocese. Nevertheless, it is natural to her energetic character to combine the role of a bishop's wife with a secular job.

Berta names three priorities when talking about her role as a bishop's wife. First, she aims to be 'a good Christian who indwells confidence to God's people and the broader society'. The family is the next priority, and trying to provide a good education for her four children. Third, the 'motherly' role of the bishop's wife in Africa is highly important. This role, she says, is primarily expressed in relation to the hospitality and travelling within the diocesan family and in leading the Mothers' Union. Berta is quick to quote 1 Timothy 3:11: 'likewise their wives must be reverent, not slanderers, temperate, faithful in all things'.

When she can, Berta likes to attend the church near their home, where the children are full members. She sees this as her spiritual home where she is made welcome and is able to share with them through times of sorrow and of joy. She is involved in a residential area prayer group, which with other groups makes up the whole congregation. This is very important to her, she says, because when she is visiting different congregations with her husband, 'I feel as a guest, meeting new people all the time.' Although she sees this as part of her Christian ministry, it is always special to be back in her spiritual home.

Berta's prayer

Almighty and merciful God, who has called men and women throughout the ages to proclaim your glory, we ask you to bless us your servants. Bless Dinis, in his duties as Bishop of Lebombo, and grant that I can be his tireless and strong helper. Bless also our children and give them health and strength in their studies. Grant that Dinis and I may guide your Church in Mozambique and promote human dignity, building a culture of peace among families, providing also jobs and professional training for your people.

Grant us this, Father, for the sake of your Son, Jesus Christ.

Amen

Esther Solomona – Sudan

Fact file

Name: Esther Solomona
Date of birth: 1942
Husband: Seme L. Solomona, Bishop of Yei, Southern Sudan
Children: Isaac, 31; Emmanuel, 28; Grace, 25; Peter, 22
First language: Bari

'The Forgotten People of Sudan' is my subtitle as I introduce Esther and her country to you. Sudan was engaged in a civil war between the north and the south from 1963 to 1971; it began again in the mid 1980s and continues to this day. There have also been periods of severe famine in the 1980s and 1990s.

The country's official name is the Republic of the Sudan. It became independent from Great Britain in 1956 and is Africa's largest country, located in the north-east. It is bordered by Egypt in the north, the Red Sea in the north-east and Libya in the north-west. Eritrea and Ethiopia are on the eastern border and Chad and the Central African Republic on the west. Finally Zaire, Uganda and Kenya border the south. It is a huge land mass, composed of an immense plain with the rock desert of the Sahara in the north, undulating sand dunes in the west and a clay plain with enormous rain forests and isolated mountains in the south and central parts.

The Bishop and I

The River Nile meanders through the country from north to south.

The population of Sudan, which is just under twenty-eight million, is predominantly young with more than two-fifths being under fifteen years of age. Life expectancy is among the lowest in the world at fifty years. Muslim Arab ethnic groups live largely in the north and central two-thirds of the country, while Sudanic people, practising animism or Christianity, live in the south. Arabic is the official language, spoken by half the population, but there are a hundred other languages. Three-quarters of the population are Muslims, less than a fifth adhere to traditional African religions and less than one tenth are Christian. Many thousands of Sudanese people now live in refugee camps in neighbouring countries because of the continuing civil war.

We have paid two official visits to Sudan. The first was over the New Year of 1993–4, when we visited the south. We were due to continue to the north but because of difficulties with the government of Sudan that plan had to be aborted.

With the war continuing, moving around was very difficult and the condition of the roads appalling. The infrastructure of the country has completely disintegrated after so many years of fighting, and the only really viable organisation is the Church, working alongside Christian aid agencies. We visited as many places as we could and were greeted with a crescendo of singing, banners of welcome and a sea of Dinka crosses high in the air. These 'Forgotten People' were so excited to have visitors and they mobbed us.

It was a very special and moving time for us and our hearts were heavy for them because of their expectation of what we could do for them – we knew we could do so little. All we could do was highlight their plight with our government on our return and shout from the rooftops, making the dreadful conditions known to those living in the West and shaking them out of their comfortable complacency and ignorance to do something. On our return George raised over £30,000 to ease the plight of the people in Sudan; he also drew attention to the problems in a speech to the House of Lords.

The visit to the north was later reinstated at the invitation of the Archbishop of Sudan, who had been bitterly disappointed at the previously cancelled one. Bishops do not have freedom to move from north to south in the country, and therefore they are never able to meet together unless they all travel out to one of the neighbouring countries. Even this is fraught with difficulties, as the government restrictions will often stop the issuing of visas to Christians.

Our visit to the north was in October 1995 following our official visit to Egypt. Although there is some infrastructure there, the conditions that the Christians have to live under are terrible. The witness of the Christians is what brought tears to my eyes, because their faith is so strong. The knowledge of God as their Father and Jesus Christ as their Saviour and the Holy Spirit guiding them is what enables them to have hope.

In spite of the difficulty of correspondence getting to Esther, we managed it, and I am so pleased because her voice is an important one to be heard. The Christians in Sudan are our brothers and sisters in the great family of the Anglican communion and they are hurting badly.

Esther Solomona

When Seme Solomona decided that he had a calling to serve God as a priest, Esther was not exactly enamoured. They had been married only a short time and she was unprepared for his decision. She quickly recognised the obstacles and problems that might lie ahead.

The Bishop and I

She recalls: 'I first looked into the life of the Church and church workers. There was no money in the Church. How were we going to feed ourselves and see to the education of our children? Priests are busy, they don't have time for their children. How am I going to face all these things?' She can remember all the thoughts that flew through her head.

'Then another side came to my mind. Let me not stand in his way and God's way. He will bring many people to God, teach them to live good lives and bring up a Christian family. And I am going to be his only wife according to the principles of Christian teaching. Above all,' she added to herself, 'God can provide for our needs. So I gave up myself to God, and later on I shared this with my husband.'

Esther has always had this strong faith and assurance, since she was a young girl. She grew up in a strong Christian family. Her mother was already a baptised Christian, and although her father was not baptised into the Church he was, in her words, 'a God-fearing man'. She was sent to attend Sunday School classes each week and began to build a picture of what God was like in her mind. She explains: 'How He looks at me, when I am doing things that are wrong. How He rejoices when I do good things.'

She began to take her faith more seriously at the age of thirteen, shortly after a spiritual experience that had an enduring impact on her life. This experience was to lead to her baptism and confirmation in August 1956. She tells the story: 'I can remember clearly one day having terrible eye problems. Then I remembered what we were told in our Sunday School, that we should pray to God when we are facing difficulties. With that little faith I went into the forest, knelt down and prayed, "Please God, could you take away the pain from my eyes? Amen." When I returned home, that very day the pain left my eyes. That incident has reminded me to this day that God hears even little children.'

Esther met Seme in 1956 during a period of civil

disturbances in south Sudan. To escape the troubles in the town, she and many others ran to a nearby village, where her future father-in-law was teaching. There she met his son and they started taking an interest in each other and became friends. Three years later they decided to marry and set a date for 1960 when Esther was eighteen.

Like all the people of southern Sudan they have experienced great troubles in their lives over many years. Esther has many times faced long periods alone, without her husband. This was sometimes because his vocation took him abroad to study, and at other times was due to the political crisis which has racked Sudan, and led to thousands of deaths. 'But always we have found God providing solutions to these problems.'

At the time of writing they and many people from southern Sudan are facing tremendous problems. Over twenty years of civil war between north and south have resulted in many deaths. The terrible toll of these years, now well documented, has been one of dreadful privation for the people of the south. Families are divided by death, famine and slavery and the Khartoum-based government, in its endeavours to fulfil a fundamentalist Islamic creed, has conducted what some describe as a jihad against Christians. Like many others from their diocese, in 1991 the Solomonas were forced to flee from their home in Yei, where they were both born and brought up. Life in exile has been a terrible strain and pressure. Esther puts it in this way: 'The problems facing the people of my diocese are those of being refugees, out of the land of their birth, with no freedom for doing what they want in their own way and no proper education for their children.' But she immediately adds: 'Nothing is bigger than the power and wisdom of God. I strongly believe we shall overcome.'

She has found great spiritual strength as a result of these experiences. In spite of all that has happened she draws her strength from counselling the many people who come to her as 'mother' of the diocese. 'From the ways they show their seriousness to be helped, I can see a deep challenge to my own spiritual pilgrimage,' she says.

The moment that Seme became a bishop in 1985, having been Dean of All Saints' Cathedral, Juba, and principal of Bishop Gwynne Theological College, Esther has found that as a woman in leadership she is treated in a similar way to her husband. She became president of the Mothers' Union in the diocese, which, as in many other developing countries, carries out a wide range of work and plays a very influential role in the lives of church women. She chairs diocesan women's meetings, counsels, organises prayer meetings and Bible studies, plans for women's activities and travels with her husband so she can meet women's groups while he pastors the men.

With a strong sense of duty, she puts her husband's needs and his work before her own, and this has not always been easy for her. They spent three years in theological college together before her husband was ordained and she says, 'I came to realise that both of us were being given a special responsibility, that demanded a lot from our lives and from our home also. I was being looked upon by other women as their leader. As a result I found that my time as a housewife and mother was being interfered with.' As Esther has already explained, since Seme has become a bishop the load on her is even heavier and there are more conflicting demands on her time, but she is confident that 'God's grace is sufficient'.

Esther's prayer in exile

Loving God, who in your time allowed your Son Jesus Christ to become a refugee, choosing Africa as His home of refuge, may you give us the same courage you gave to Joseph and Mary so that we may not lose hope in you. May you help us to return to our own country as you returned Jesus to His home.

Bless our days in exile, so that we may not forget you. In Jesus' name we pray,

Amen

Russelle Thompson – USA

Fact file

Name: Russelle Cross Thompson
Date of birth: 7 January 1942
Husband: Herbert Thompson, Jnr, Bishop of the diocese
of Southern Ohio
Children: Herbert R. Thompson, 29; Owen C.
Thompson, 27; Kyrie R. Thompson, 19

I first met Russelle in 1992. We were doing an official
visit to several dioceses in the USA and the diocese of
Southern Ohio was one of them. We were there only a
short time. My husband gave a lecture, and then we went
to the home of Herbert and Russelle for a dinner party. I
distinctly remember that Russelle had a cold and a sore
throat and it was then that I found out that she was a
professional singer. Naturally she was worried about this
infection as she was going to sing after the meal. Russelle
did manage to give us a short rendition and I realised what
a wonderful gift God had given her and how much joy she
gives to others by using it to His glory.

We have met several times since, latterly in New York
at the 300th anniversary of Trinity Church, Wall Street.
There was a wonderful celebration on Ellis Island, which
was for many years the entry point for all those arriving in
the New World. I happened to bump into Russelle among

the 1100 guests on this great occasion. We exchanged a few words, mainly about Herbert's nomination for the post of presiding bishop – not a post that anybody would actually want to fill, but if colleagues felt it would be right to stand, Herbert and Russelle would pray about it and only then would he allow his name to go forward.

Such is the spirituality of Herbert and Russelle and their togetherness in ministry.

Wherever Russelle is called to live, she will very soon make an impact on the community, and her singing will give her an entry into other people's lives, bringing joy to them as it does to her. I am pleased she has shared her story with us. Her optimism and joy shine through.

Russelle Thompson

'When we were in our second parish, I was asked by a woman, "What do you do?" I answered: "I am raising our children," to which she replied: "Is that all, you don't work outside the home?" And on and on she went,' Russelle recalls.

'My mother was visiting us and overheard this conversation. After the woman left and I was feeling as useless as a piece of lint on a new dress, she turned to me and said, "I have never seen one woman work as hard as you do. Don't let anyone make out you are less of a person because you do not work outside the home!" '

Russelle counts herself lucky to have been able to be with her children during their growing-up years and also to have had a career or ministry as a singer, teacher, chef and entrepreneur. Furthermore, she says frankly: 'My husband's ministry has always been mine. It is our ministry and has been for the last twenty-seven years.'

The great love of Russelle's life is singing. She has sung at

Carnegie Hall, Radio City Music Hall and Judson Hall. She
has been on television and performed for radio audiences.
It was at the age of seven that she first joined a choir.

She was the eldest of three girls born to Doris and
Owen Cross. Her father worked for New York City
Fire Department as a firefighter. 'He was one of the
first African-Americans to break the colour barrier,' she
explains. 'He was probably the most unique person I have
ever met. There were so many different qualities about him.
He had a pure gentleness about him that only he possessed.
He had a sense of humour that you just can't find any more.
My father could make you laugh so much that the tears
would be streaming down your face,' she recalls fondly. 'My
mother worked for the New York City Health Department,
in the Bureau of Records as a clerk. She was my best friend,
the wind beneath my wings. She always went out of her way
to help those around her; she was a gift to us all. My daughter
says she remembers that her Dee Dee always had a smile on
her face. She was a woman of independence, style and a
rare grace.'

Russelle has fond memories of her grandmother, Louise,
who lived with the family in a fifth-floor walk-up in
Manhattan. Russelle and her sisters, Paula and Gail, were
'sixth-generation Episcopalians'. They attended St Philip's
church in Harlem and were all active in the church. Russelle
sang in the choir and taught in the Sunday School.

'We attended a Christian camp, Camp Minisink, in
upstate New York. My husband's camp was the sister
camp to mine, as I found out later during our courtship.
We still battle over which camp was best (naturally mine
was). The wonderful thing about Camp Minisink was its
year-round programme that was a major influence on my
life. During my childhood and teenage years, helped by my
parents, church and camp, I was learning what it meant to
grow into the stature of Christ.'

When she left school, Russelle studied at the New York School of Business. She also studied music with the Lola Hayes and Jonathan Brice Studios. She worked for the New York Mission Society for nine years.

Herbert Thompson was made a deacon in June 1965 and sent to St Gabriel's, New York, as a vicar to oversee its eventual closing. His first service as a priest was at the Christmas Eve service, which he wanted to be a very special occasion for his flock, family and friends. He decided to have a choir and had to call upon a friend to get together some singers, since St Gabriel's only had a small congregation.

'Our first rehearsal was held and the Rev. Herbert Thompson Jnr arrived to meet us. I remember he was wearing a grey suit and was accompanied by a toy French poodle, also grey and wearing a rhinestone collar (the poodle, not Herb). We married on 28 September 1968 and we have been singing, more or less in tune, for thirty years,' she says proudly.

A whole new world opened up to Russelle when she married a clergyman. 'We have travelled around the world, and visited places most people only read about. We have met people from all walks of life: royalty, presidents, governors, governor-generals, mayors, Archbishop Desmond Tutu and three Archbishops of Canterbury and many people who are not well known, who are working as Christian men and women wherever they happen to be. I feel humble and honoured to be able to share in my husband's ministry and it has enriched my life a thousandfold,' she says.

Russelle has found that her job description has changed since becoming a bishop's wife. Now the children are older, they need her in different ways. She no longer teaches Sunday School or is a camp counsellor or manager of the Church Thrift Shop she helped found (with an income of $30,000 a year), and she doesn't have to cook as much as she used to. 'There are always entrepreneurial opportunities around the corner, but for now I am still able to fulfil my main ministry, which is to stand by my husband and represent God's people in the diocese of Southern Ohio and sing God's praises to the best of my ability,' she declares.

'My time is your time, your time is my time,' is a song lyric Russelle uses to describe the conflicting demands on her time. Just before she met Herbert she can remember saying how bored she was and how she wished she could travel. The prayer was answered: she met Herbert and has not been bored since. Furthermore, they have travelled all over the place, to the extent that their theme song has become 'On the Road Again'.

'We enjoy the busy-ness of our lives,' she says. 'But it does have its down side.' These are the kinds of things they find themselves saying to each other all the time: 'Gee, I just checked my date book and we have an opening for dinner three months from now'; 'But I thought we might have a few days in between just for ourselves'; 'Give me those dates so I can make sure we can move something around'; 'You're having another dinner meeting, but I've planned this wonderful dinner. Oh, you mean we have a dinner tonight and tomorrow night too?'; 'I've set some time to clean the house and to do some gardening in the year 2010!'

Nevertheless, where she used to have hands-on relationships with parishioners in the past she finds this is missing now. There are eighty-seven parishes in the diocese and it takes about two years to visit them all. Another effect of being a bishop's wife is the exposure to the Church at large. This has been both a bane and a blessing, she says. 'On the down side, watching some of our priests and bishops forgetting they were chosen by God to serve Him has been hard to take. On the blessing side, there are wonderful things taking place in the Anglican communion, which gives me hope for us all,' she says.

Russelle Thompson – USA

Herbert and Russelle have travelled to their companion diocese of Ijebu in the province of Nigeria in the last twelve years to take part in mission opportunities. They are now entering another three-way 'companionship' with the Maori diocese of Aotearoa and New Zealand and with the diocese of the Windward Islands. 'One cannot help but think and feel that God is in His Heaven and all is well with the world,' she says.

She is similarly full of optimism for the diocese of Southern Ohio. In the past the diocese has been a leading force in the Episcopal Church. Forward Movement Publications started there, together with other episcopal charities, including the Presiding Bishop's Fund for World Relief. There are four retirement homes in the diocese, and the Church Army (a street evangelism arm of the Church) is highly active there too.

'Today we are embracing our mission of proclaiming Christ (you might say that Southern Ohio is not one to let a good opportunity pass us by). We have almost reached our goal in our nine-million-dollar Capital Campaign Fund, which will help to build new churches, help existing congregations, empower diocesan programmes for youth, develop an Anglican Academy for lay and clergy Christian education, build a conference centre and refurbish our diocese camp.

'We also now have a cathedral at the centre of the diocese. We are working to strengthen the clergy and their families for service. Our people have had the opportunity to support a vision brought to them by their bishop. They have shared that vision and now most of the vision and its programmes are in place.'

Russelle knows that there is a loneliness in leadership. She does not have a regular place of worship and sometimes feels isolated. But she says that clergy lives are all isolated from Day One. 'We seek help for our children, but not for our relationship between husband and wife. We are supposed to have it right. Unless there is a catastrophe, one does not talk to the priest down the street or to the bishop. The priest is a colleague and the bishop is the person who has power over your vocation. I am not sure the places where we worship can help us, but thank God for families,' she says.

Russelle finds her spiritual strength in God's creation. She stops and looks around her at cloud formations or sunsets or the way it rains on one side of the road and not on the other. This, she finds, reassures her that God is alive, well and near to her.

What has she learnt since becoming a bishop's wife? 'I have learnt that I can make people nervous just by walking into a room. I have learnt that I can be in a church with a lot of people and still be in a pew all by myself. I have learnt that I will always be first in line at a confirmation reception in the parish house. I have learnt that I am now the bishop's lovely wife and not the rector's lovely wife. I have learnt that once again I am at the head table and alone. I have learnt that the beautiful altar flowers are mine to take home. I have learnt I can have a special seat at consecrations. I have learnt that in Africa I am the mother of the diocese and I have learnt of God's great love for His children and that I am one of them, and that in Nigeria a young girl will fall to her knees when she is introduced to me. I have learnt that it is impossible to keep on a diet.

'All in all,' she concludes, 'I am well taken care of and much loved.'

Russelle's prayer

Gracious God, bless us with your presence in this family's home and in our lives. Strengthen our hearts to love you as well as each other. Give us the grace to continue to be a strong family and proclaim you to be the head of this household. Fill this house with love and help us to be an example to a world in chaos, where broken homes have begun to outnumber families still together. Use us as instruments of your peace and let us find strength and solace in you and in each other.

In your holy name,

Amen

Julia Yong – Sabah

Fact file

Name: Julia Yong
Date of birth: 7 July 1942
Husband: Rt Rev. Datuk Yong Ping Chung, Bishop of
  Sabah, South East Asia
Children: Sarah Miriam Yong Oi Tsun; Lois Elizabeth
  Yong Khin Tsun

When I first met Julia, in November 1993, we were on an
official visit to the dioceses of South East Asia, namely
West Malaysia, Sarawak, Sabah and Singapore, in order
to facilitate their discussions towards forming a province.
Christianity is a minority religion in all these countries, but
in each place Christians have freedom to worship and in their
commitment to Christ to be active in education, health and
other social-work projects.

In Sabah we stayed in the home of Bishop Yong Ping
Chung and Julia Yong and had a wonderful time with them
and their congregations.

November is the rainy season and there had been heavy
rains. As part of the arranged programme we were to travel
into the interior, where an enormous youth camp was being
held to train young men and women in evangelism. There
was to be a big service and George was to celebrate and
preach.

On the day we were to leave, the bishop was looking very preoccupied. He had heard that the roads we were to travel on were flooded in places and could be impassable by the time we reached them if the rains continued. However, we set out in faith in a Land-Rover with Julia and Ping Chung, who was driving. We arrived without mishap at the guest house where we were to stay overnight, nestled under Mt Kinabalu. This is the highest mountain in Sabah, very popular with professional climbers but also very dangerous, particularly in the wet season. It was a couple of months later that a British Army expedition went tragically wrong on that very mountain.

We set off early the next morning for the youth camp and had a hair-raising journey, with some parts of the road partly swept away and extremely dangerous to pass. By the grace of God and very skilful driving we got there, to a tumultuous welcome from the young people.

The service started and the rains came down. Not a problem if you are worshipping in a building, but we were under a huge canvas structure. As the rain got heavier the canvas dipped under the weight of the water. Young men started rushing around with long poles to push up the canvas and send the water off the edges and into the concrete drainage channels around the main seating area. Meanwhile the service continued. It got to the point for the sermon, when George was preaching, and the rain became even heavier. His voice got louder in order to try and drown out the incessant drumming on the canvas, but he could not beat the elements. No one could hear. Eventually he said, 'I have never before had to compete with the rain and I am losing! Let us carry on with the Eucharist and have the sermon after, when hopefully the rain will have eased or ceased.'

Julia and I were sitting by the side of one of the drainage channels. As more water was pushed off the canvas it got fuller and fuller, and we had to raise our feet or they would have been in the water. Miraculously as the service continued the rain began to get lighter. The sermon was preached without challenge, and by the end the sun was shining. What a privilege it was to spend time with hundreds of enthusiastic young people, giving a year of their lives for the sake of the gospel without being paid, receiving just their keep from wherever they were sent by the Church.

We survived the dangerous journey back on the water-logged roads, relieved and very pleased that we had managed to honour our commitment.

Under the leadership of Ping Chung and Julia Sabah is a missionary diocese, committed to the growth of the Church in this Decade of Evangelism and a wonderful example, in a country where Christianity is a minority religion, of a steady growth without giving offence to other faith communities. One of the most significant initiatives undertaken by Sabah is Mission One-One-Three, which has been an inspiration to Anglicans throughout the world. It is a simple formula by which every churchgoer is asked to bring at least one non-Christian to faith every three years. With such a modest but radical target the Church is growing rapidly.

It is a pleasure to have Julia as a contributor to this book.

Julia Yong

'Much of my childhood is a blur to me – like a dream of someone else's life, not mine. I have crossed and re-crossed different cultures, languages and a variety of lifestyles. I thank God for the richness of my past. It will always remain as one great big blessing from God.'

Julia Yong was born in the war-torn years of the Second

World War in southern China. Her father was a priest, involved in the care of refugees. He travelled into often very dangerous territory and decided it was best for his family to stay with his wife's parents near Canton.

When Julia was only five they moved to Hong Kong, where her father became the rector of St Mary's Church, Causeway Bay. She describes her father as a 'godly' man, who sacrificed much to his vocation. The Church needed funds and her parents offered the rent money intended for their flat. They moved into the small choir changing-room in the church building. With four children there was simply not enough room, so the decision was taken to send Julia and her elder sister, May, to boarding schools. This was the beginning of her life as a boarder, and she continued in a succession of schools and universities for years.

There was also to be a succession of moves for the whole family. Her father felt called by God to serve in Malaysia (then Malaya), but first decided to take up a scholarship to study at Canterbury in England. Julia's mother went ahead to study English and a year later her father took his four children on a long 'cruise' from Hong Kong to Italy and then by train to England. 'Remembering those days, I really admire my father for coping with us four very young active children. I can still remember that, even on the ship, my father never stopped doing God's work. He started church services on board and with the help of a Christian woman, who later became an important part of my life in America, he started a Sunday School.'

After Julia's father finished his studies in England, the family travelled in dribs and drabs to the United States of America. May and Julia finished their school year first and then followed on the *Queen Elizabeth*. In America an elderly well-established Bostonian couple offered to take up guardianship of May and Julia, and an Episcopalian boarding school run by the Sisters of St

Anne in Massachusetts offered to give the two girls a good education.

Seeing that the girls were well provided for, the rest of the family went off to Malaya to start their ministry there. 'I feel that this was the real breaking point in my life separating East and West,' comments Julia. 'I stayed on the North American continent until I finished my university. May and I went back to the Orient only once during those years, for a few weeks during a summer break from university.

'These were very mixed years. We were assimilated into the American culture and lifestyle. We became a part of everyone who looked after us. We had many caring "mothers" and "fathers". Although May and I never really had a home, all tried their best to provide one for us. I will always be grateful to God for all my guardians, the convent and all the "adopted parents" for their love. We were brought up as one of them, as proper young ladies, well-sheltered and protected, with good Christian teaching and social graces. Outwardly my life was what others would have dreamed about, everything on a silver platter, but inwardly those were very lonely years.'

Julia recalls how tough and lonely it was to fit into everyone's life and lifestyle. She tried to bury the loneliness by living a fantasy. 'Everything appeared wonderful on the surface. Only years later through prayer counselling did I come to terms and face to face with my past. Only then did I realise that God had always been there for me. Although I had no earthly anchor, He was my anchor.'

She now thanks God for the richness of her past and the experiences she had in her youth. She also remembers her parents with love and gratitude, knowing that they never stopped loving her and praying for her. 'I can thank God that because we belonged to the world-wide family, many wonderful Christian brothers and sisters stretched out their loving hands to me. Indeed, I was never alone.'

Julia Yong – Sabah

Her father was appointed as the Assistant Bishop of Singapore and Malaya in the late 1950s and it was later, in 1965, that he was called to be the Bishop of Sabah. After Julia had finished studying at a Canadian university, she decided to visit her parents. What started off as a temporary visit of a month lasted a year.

Even though her father had been born in Sabah (British North Borneo), to Julia it was just a place on the map. She recalls having twenty-nine injections against almost every disease that the health department could find in the book. 'Sabah seemed like the end of the earth, a place where only extremely adventurous people would go. I was excited not only at the adventure but also at the opportunity of finding myself.'

She soon found herself in work: when one of the teachers from the mission school went on leave to Australia, Julia took over her matriculation classes. She found Sabah a fascinating place, but fitted in like a tourist or expatriate. She had no intention of staying because she didn't feel she belonged. 'Asia was no longer my home,' she explains.

But it was during this year that her husband-to-be came back to Sabah. He had been studying in Newfoundland, Canada, and came home for the summer to keep in touch with the needs of the people and the Church in Sabah. 'We became friends easily and it was good, especially for me, to be able to relate to someone in English who knew something about America and Canada. We found that we had a lot to talk about.'

However, for Julia it was not love at first sight. Marriage was the furthest thing from her mind. First, she had never wanted to be a priest's wife. At this stage, she says, she was still far away from God and didn't want to be part of the Church. Second, she couldn't speak any of the local languages. Third, she couldn't tolerate the heat and didn't feel at home in Sabah. Finally, 'we were as different as night and day'.

In most cases this list of reasons might have prevented things going any further. But Ping Chung proved to be a formidable man. Julia recalls, 'Ping Chung knew that I was the helpmate and partner that God had provided for him in his life and his ministry. After he left to go back to Canada, he wrote faithfully almost every day. The first thing he did was to work on my faith. Every letter was almost like a sermon!'

She returned at the end of the year to the convent in Boston, feeling totally confused. Not long after, Ping Chung attended a youth conference in the area and they met up. After much talking and praying and trying to work things out, he took Julia into a church and proposed. Six months later they were married in St Anne's Convent, the place where she grew up. Her father and mother came after the 1968 Lambeth Conference to perform the ceremony. Best of all, the whole family was gathered there for the occasion, one of those very rare times when they were all together.

Julia spent the final year of Ping Chung's training with him in Newfoundland, with the looming prospect of leaving the security of North America and facing the unknown in Sabah.

Everyone was excited to have Ping Chung back. He was the first local to be trained overseas and to come back to the diocese. At the time Sabah was staffed by dedicated missionaries from other parts of the world. The people of the diocese were looking forward to the return of one of their own, who could speak their languages and understand their cultures. A lot was expected of him and he was eager and ready to get started.

A lot was also expected of Julia. She went to Sabah with an 'expectant heart'. 'Although I didn't know what the future would hold, I wanted and was eager to be a help to Ping Chung in the Church. We were ready to settle down, to have a family and to establish a "home". But it was difficult leaving America. At that time I never thought I would ever have a chance to visit again. Leaving America meant leaving everything behind, crossing cultures again, as I did seventeen years ago, and starting over again. It meant cutting whatever ties I had in the past.

'But in America, although I was considered a "member of the family" in whichever home I was in, I knew deep inside me I didn't really belong. Therefore cutting ties meant facing reality. I felt a great void as I realised that I didn't really have anyone to belong to in America. Going to Sabah meant establishing a home base. I was frightened, but excited.'

The early years proved to be a very difficult time of adjustment. She was coming back to Sabah, not as a visitor but as part of the country and the people. She desperately wanted to fit in. She says, 'I knew everyone was happy with Ping Chung, but right from the start I felt I was a disappointment to them. I felt I wasn't accepted by the people. I couldn't speak any of the local languages and they couldn't understand and accept that, because they knew my parents and that they were very Chinese. As I could speak only English, the language of the old colonial masters and educated people, many thought I was too proud or snobbish to speak a local dialect. Although I was Chinese I was brought up in America. I made many mistakes because I didn't understand or have much knowledge of the local customs and traditions. Everyone expected me to know everything, thinking I was away overseas to study for just a few years and had come back "Westernised".'

She met with criticism and discouragement, trying hard to relearn Chinese but finding that she was having to learn from scratch. Sometimes she felt proud of herself when she had learnt a new word or phrase, only to find that her effort was not well received when she tried it out. She longed for the words of praise which the foreign missionaries got when they tried to say only one word in a local dialect. She spent hours in tears and became depressed. On the surface she was trying to present a happy, cheerful appearance, but her inner feelings were too painful to expose and face, even for herself.

Ping Chung was very supportive and tried his best to encourage. But he was very busy and away from home a lot. Within a year of being in Sabah, the diocese had no bishop and only a handful of priests. Julia's father had been commissioned by the then Archbishop of Canterbury to start the new diocese of West Malaysia and missionaries had to leave because of immigration problems. So Ping Chung and a few other priests were left. Besides starting Chinese work in the cathedral, he had to travel throughout the diocese because of the lack of priests. Julia felt like a liability rather than a help. She was 'miserable, alone and broken'.

'It was in this state of desperation that I turned to God for help. It was then, broken before God, that I realised that I had never really known Him personally nor experienced His mighty power and love. Even after Ping Chung had brought me back to God I never did surrender myself totally to Him.

'I thought I had received the Lord Jesus into my life, but I really hadn't. I had a lot of head knowledge. I was very sincere in my desire to serve God, but I was still very much in control of my own life. I wanted to do good, and even though I was doing everything in the name of Christianity, I was doing it for myself. I repented before God. I began to let go of myself and to allow God to take over. I opened my life to Jesus and surrendered to Him. It was the beginning of a long learning process.'

Julia now looks back on these painful early days in Sabah

as the prelude to a strengthened faith. She remembers clearly the realisation that God cared for her and loved her and taught her what it means to surrender to Him. As a result she began to worry less about being accepted and learnt to be happy in Him. Not that things became rosy overnight. There were still growing pains, but she began to understand what God meant when He said to Paul, 'My grace is sufficient for you, for my power is made perfect in weakness.'

A thirst for knowledge of the Bible and theological study followed naturally from this discovery of the love and sufficiency of God. She enrolled in a theological course so that she could be more disciplined and systematic in her voracious and urgent search of the Bible. 'Instead of waiting for people to accept me, I decided to accept and to love the place and the people. I tried harder to adapt to this new country which I now considered my home. By God's help I started to be less sensitive to criticism, ridicules and misunderstandings as I tried to pick up the languages and learn about the cultures. This was a slow and agonising process, that I am still learning. However, a big black cloud seemed to be slowly lifting from my life.' Eventually, with two little daughters, she found for the first time that, with Ping Chung, the family felt like a team.

Having confronted and overcome such difficulties in her early life and ministry, becoming a bishop's wife in 1990 was not the greatest change she had ever experienced. But being married to a bishop, she believes, is a calling from God. In the same way that God called Ping Chung to be Bishop of Sabah, He also called Julia to be his helpmate.

'My place is to be by my husband, to be his wife, the mother of our children, his companion, his sounding board and foremost his prayer supporter and partner. I travel with him as much as possible to official diocesan events. On the personal level, I try to help him to be in touch with the family and personal affairs, looking after little details that he doesn't have time for. I try to encourage him to take time off and to relax. I like to make our home open and welcoming.'

Julia does a great deal of work with women and with wives of clergy and church workers. Such women leaders, she says, have tremendous ministries in the parishes. She sees her role as an encourager and listener to them. She tries to go to their homes and share their family life, taking great delight when some of the children call her 'Grandma'.

Julia describes her daily devotions as a 'need' to be alone with God. She sets a time early in the morning to pray and resubmit herself to God's will. She also finds her daily prayer time with Ping Chung essential. As a couple they are grateful for the prayers of their children, the people of the diocese and the world-wide prayers of the Church. 'I still have a long way to go in this area, but I know our loving God will continue to lead me deeper and deeper into His sanctuary,' declares Julia.

Julia's prayer

Dear Gracious and Heavenly Father, we praise you and worship you. We bow down before you and submit to your sovereignty. Thank you for your love for us. Thank you for your salvation through Jesus Christ. Thank you for the Holy Spirit, our inspirer. We thank you for the universal Church and thank you for your grace that we can be part of your family. Bring us into greater and greater experience of the reality of your love. Help us to share that love with those around us and beyond.

Father, we thank you for our diocese. Thank you for the uniqueness and the richness of our land and the varieties of races, languages and customs. In you, we are one in the bond of love through your Son, Jesus. Keep us in unity as we serve you and your people.

Thank you for the vision of Mission One-One-Three. Father, we know it is your desire for everyone to come into the fullness of your grace. Help us to be bold for you and to be obedient to your will. Father, we want to learn from you and to be open to the guidance of your Holy Spirit. You are the potter and we are the clay. Forgive us when we fall short of your expectations.

Continue to give us strength, courage and wisdom to share your love with everyone. May your name be lifted up and glorified and praised.

Through Jesus Christ our Lord,

Amen

Postscript:
Susie Chang Him – Seychelles

Fact file

Name: Susie Chang Him
Date of birth: 10 June 1953
Died: 9 May 1996
Husband: French Chang Him, Bishop of the Seychelles, province of the Indian Ocean
Children: Twins, Frances and Michelle, 21

This chapter needs little introduction. It is in memory of Susie, to whom the book is dedicated. She died before she could tell her story.

I remember Susie from the Lambeth Conference of 1988. She must have been one of the youngest spouses at the conference because she was only thirty-four years of age. French, her husband, was Bishop of the Seychelles and Primate of the Indian Ocean. That has a wonderful ring about it! It means a collection of dioceses which form one province and are in the geographical area of the Indian Ocean, with French Chang Him as the then senior bishop.

We visited the Seychelles in June 1993 and the other countries in the province. On our final evening we had a meal with French and Susie in their home and celebrated Susie's fortieth birthday. Little did we know, when we left the next day and Susie waved us off from the tarmac, that we would not see her again, at least not on this earth.

The previous evening we had been talking about them coming to London with their twin girls for a sabbatical and staying with us at Lambeth Palace, where we have a small apartment for such use. We were all very excited by the prospect of this happening. The Seychelles is very isolated from any other land mass, so it is important for the bishop to have the opportunity outside his own church for fellowship and sharing of ideas and learning from others. We were hoping to arrange this for French and Susie.

I had the idea for this book already burning inside and talked to Susie about it. In my plan I knew I wanted her to be a contributor but it was still in the embryonic stage within me, without even a publisher. When the idea began to become a reality and I was able to trawl my mind for willing contributors, Susie's was the first name on my list. She replied enthusiastically, confirming she would like to tell her story. She was at that time in remission from the terrible ravages of the cancer which had invaded her.

However, Susie became too weak to do it and died without putting pen to paper. I knew in my heart that her story was important for this book; French, with Frances and Michelle, consented to write their story of a loving wife and mother and her achievements for the people and especially the children of the Seychelles.

There are no changes in the chapter that follows. It is exactly as French, Frances and Michelle have written it.

Susie Chang Him

Susie's life

'I'm going to tell them everything!' There was a mischievous twinkle in her eyes. In response, I gave her an enquiring look. She continued: 'You know that Eileen has asked me to contribute a chapter to a book on bishops' wives that she is putting together for the next Lambeth Conference? I shall tell them how we met, everything. Do you mind?'

'I thought you had already done that at the last Lambeth Conference in '88. No, I don't mind, go ahead, tell them everything.'

The above conversation took place in March 1996. Susie lay in bed in the Victoria Hospital here in Seychelles. I had just come back from Nairobi, where I had been attending a meeting entitled 'Conférence Internationale sur l'Anglicanisme d'Expression Français dans la communion Anglicane'. One of the matters we had discussed there was the importance that the bishops from the francophone churches make their voices heard at Lambeth 1998.

The curious thing was that I had suddenly felt strangely unwell as I was packing to return home. Immediately, I said to myself: 'Something is wrong at home.' When I telephoned a short time later, Michelle, one of our twin daughters, said: 'Mummy has been taken to hospital. She was having some pain. But she does not want you to worry.'

The heavy cloud which had descended upon me that Sunday afternoon in Kenya was to prove to be more than a passing cloud.

In November 1993 Susie was diagnosed as having carcinoma of the stomach and she was advised to undergo total gastrectomy immediately. This was followed by radiotherapy in the island of Réunion near Mauritius and chemotherapy back in Seychelles. She resumed work in July 1995, feeling mentally her former self but physically considerably less strong. The relapse came in March 1996 and she was called to be with the Lord on 9 May 1996, aged forty-two years.

The police estimated that about two thousand people attended Susie's funeral, which took place in St Paul's Cathedral, Victoria, on Saturday 11 May. She was laid to rest in the family cemetery at Bel Ombre about three miles away. Although the funeral was at 3 p.m. it was not until after 5 p.m. that the burial could take place. The number of cars and coaches that made their way to the village cemetery was overwhelming. Most of the local tour operators offered coaches gratis to transport the many mourners. There were about fifteen coaches in all.

What caused the funeral of this petite wife and mother, born in Arusha Chinni, Tanzania, of Seychelles parents on 10 June 1953, to become almost a national occasion? Many of the children who did not know me by name called me 'Miss Susie's husband'. And I loved it. The children knew her because she had co-ordinated the School Dental Service for the whole of Seychelles. Hundreds of them will have had their first experience in the dental chair with Susie as their dentist. This School Dental Service undertakes most of the dental treatment for young people from the time their baby teeth appear up to the age of eighteen years. As a hygienist, Susie's work at the dental clinic also extended to adults. She managed to build a kind of trust, mixed with a professional but friendly rapport with all those she treated. She loved her work and saw it as a vocation, using the skills God had given her to relieve pain and promote dental health of the highest quality possible.

Seychelles being a small country of some 72,000 inhabitants, Susie was soon known through direct contact with people, especially through her frequent television or radio programmes in connection with her work. Some of her closest friends were handicapped children with different disabilities who needed extra care when being treated.

Her activities in the community were also extensive. She sang in the National Choir, was a member of the Soroptimists, took part in sponsored walks and runs in support of various charities, and was vice-chairperson of the Seychelles Broadcasting Corporation.

In the parish she sang in the choir, taught in church school, and was a member of the liturgical group and of the Mothers' Union. She had also served on the parish church council.

Family history

Susie's father, Ernest Talma, started his working life as a teacher. He emigrated to Tanzania in the 1940s and worked as a mechanic. He married Elina Nalletamby, née Marie, a widow with four young daughters. Susie was the second of three children by the second marriage. She had a twin brother who died in infancy. She and her elder sister and younger brother were sent to school in Seychelles in 1960, about a year before the then Tanganyika became independent, because of political unrest and fear of possible violence following independence. She had attended the Aga Khan Kindergarten in Tanzania and did her primary education in St Paul's Girls' School, Seychelles. Through her hard work, she won a scholarship to study at the only grammar school for girls at the time, the Renina Mundi Convent, run by the Roman Catholic Sisters of St Joseph of Cluny.

During her schooling, she and her siblings stayed with an aunt, who had a family of five, all boys. After completing her studies at the convent school, she worked as a student nurse in the Victoria Hospital before proceeding to New Zealand with another colleague from the same school to train as a dental therapist. They went as pioneers of a new scheme and both qualified in 1973. Susie undertook two further training courses. The first was at Guy's Hospital in London in 1978 to train as a dental hygienist; the second was with the South Australian Dental School, to equip her to assist in establishing the School Dental Service training scheme in Seychelles. Susie also did some attachments with the School of Dentistry, Umea University, Sweden.

Professionally, she attained the post of Assistant Director of Dental Services and retained her responsibilities as the Co-ordinator of the School Dental Service simultaneously.

At the time of her death she had been researching, with two Swedish dentists, a project on the oral health of the child population in Seychelles and the oral health of the adult population. The survey work, carried out in 1993 and 1994, involved checking and interviewing several hundred people selected at random, some of whom she visited at home after working hours. The two works were continued by her Swedish colleagues and published posthumously in 1997. One of the Swedes described the project on the child population as 'Susie's baby'. She was the initiator and project leader.

Family life

I had known Susie since I returned to Seychelles in 1963 after theological training in England. She was then a ten-year-old smiling young girl who used to come and spend her holidays with her grandparents on the island of Praslin, where I was parish priest. We fell in love ten years later when she returned to Seychelles after her studies in New Zealand. That was in February, and I was due to leave for Canada in the September of that year for post-ordination training at Trinity College, University of Toronto. Perhaps rather selfishly I felt time was not on my side. I was then thirty-seven years old. We got engaged a week before I left for Toronto. It was going to be a very long ten months apart. Only a month after I returned we got married, on 20 July 1975.

Shipwreck

Two weeks after our marriage, the boat on which I was travelling from Praslin to the main island, Mahe, capsized in heavy seas, and we were afloat for six hours in the ocean before being rescued. Susie, who was well when she had gone to work that morning, suddenly felt sick for no apparent reason and returned home to rest. Soon she was to know why. The Job's Comforter who came to break the news of the shipwreck added: 'I understand there are no survivors.' Later we gave thanks that it was just the opposite. We were all rescued. That shipwreck was to make Susie and me realise even more the very close bond which existed between us – of a telepathic nature – which was to manifest itself in so many ways in the twenty years ahead.

The incident also brought home to me the truth that Jesus is alive. He was with me in the deep. I felt His presence in a most powerful way, which brought an unusual kind of peace in the midst of the storm in which I was caught.

Frances and Michelle

Our twin daughters, Frances Cynthia and Michelle Susan, were born on 6 October 1976. Both Susie and I felt we had been living on borrowed life. She and the twins lived because of the skills of the gynaecologist and the Lord's grace and mercy. I was in Praslin the night of their birth and 'saw' Susie between life and death. I was on my knees. I should have been there with her, but there was no way of making the journey across in the middle of the night.

Frances and Michelle, identical physically but not in terms of character, have brought us so much joy and blessing.

Now, at the age of twenty and having just completed their pre-university studies, they hope to travel overseas to further their education, since there are no universities in our country.

These are their own testimonies about their mother only a short time after she died:

Frances: It is almost seven months since Mum left us and yet it seems like yesterday. Yesterday, because we are still being reconciled to the fact that we cannot see her any more. It is hard to believe that it has really happened, in so short a time. Losing Mum has been like losing a part of myself. For nineteen years she had been supporting, loving, educating and caring for us. To me, she was everything a mother could be. She was so understanding and supportive. If I was in doubt or confused about something, Mum was always prepared to listen and allay my doubts. When I was down, she would say or do something funny to make me laugh and brighten me up. She was always more concerned about the needs and welfare of others than herself.

One thing which really impressed me during Mum's illness, and always will, was the beautiful smile she wore most of the time. This openly showed how great her inner strength was. Her faith touched many hearts. In spite of her obvious pain and discomfort, she smiled at us from her sick bed. Even in her distress, she was comforting and reassuring us.

Her illness was not only a painful experience, but it helped us learn some very important lessons. The first was about love. She proved her love for us to the last. We have also learnt that we must never give up, even when things seem at their worst. We prayed and hoped Mum would recover, but it was not to be. God had other plans. She was needed elsewhere. So we had to let her go. It was painful, but we know she is closer to us now than she ever was before. Besides, she is not suffering any more.

Michelle: My first recollection of Mummy was when I was about four years old. She used to take us to the playground and we had fun together. However, what made Frances and me jealous was seeing little children running to her. At that age neither of us knew much about handicapped children and we did not like to see Mummy paying a lot of attention to them. But as we grew up, she helped us understand children with disabilities and how much they needed affection and being understood and loved like the rest of us.

Mum was always there when we needed her. At night, she and Dad would tell us bedtime stories. She would nurse us when we were sick and she really took care of me when, as a small girl, I fell and damaged my two front teeth. Even though she was a dentist, she used to give us sweets when we were not well. But, of course, at night she made sure we brushed our teeth properly.

One thing Mum always wanted us to be since we were small was to be well disciplined. She was always proud of us when we did things right and took part in school activities.

Growing into adolescents was the time we needed Mum most and she was always there for us. I cannot think of a better mother who could have given better advice than she did. We never felt shy to ask her about anything. She would always tell us about her past and how life was when she was our age.

Whenever we felt down, Mum was there to cheer us up. At times we disagreed. But we knew her well enough to know we could only go so far and no further!

Concerning our education, she was always concerned about how we were doing in class. She assisted us with our homework as much as she could and made sure we completed it before school the following day.

Since Mummy first went into hospital, Frances and I

missed her coming home from work and asking how things had gone at school. We miss all the fun we used to have together and the pet names which she called us. She used to dance and sing when she was happy.

We thank her for helping us to be who we are now. We know she has left us at a young age, but we have learnt so much from her. Now it is our turn to face the future before us and to put into practice all she has taught us.

'I have done it!'

At the Lambeth Conference in 1988, Susie told me how the bishops' wives had been asked to share in their group about husband/wife relationships. She explained how she had mentioned that we were very different in so many ways. 'I described us in this way,' she said. 'When French says, "We need to think and pray about it," I often answer, "I've already done it!"'

I was to discover how much this had characterised a number of things Susie had undertaken. She initiated the formation of, and nurtured, two groups, the Anglican Health Workers' Fellowship and a church group called Lespwar (Creole for 'hope') which was aimed at bringing single mothers together for fellowship, support and spiritual nurture, after someone had mentioned the need for those two groups to exist. Our family was to discover that she had made provision for us and the future in a number of ways, which touched us deeply when we realised after her departure what she had done.

Commitment

When we got married, I was an archdeacon. Neither of us knew that I was to be called to assume responsibility for both the diocese and the province in the course of our existence together. The transition from one office to another, no doubt, had direct implications for Susie herself and the family. Her support and allegiance was absolute, for which I was deeply grateful and by which I was strengthened. In such an isolated part of the world, where your nearest episcopal colleague and his wife are a thousand miles of ocean away, mutual support between a bishop and his spouse cannot be overemphasised. Susie understood that. But it also placed an extra weight on her.

By nature, we were different in many ways. We had to work through quite a number of different issues, at times difficult ones, in our marriage and our respective professions together. After twenty years we had learnt some very important lessons, sometimes the hard way, but we also felt we had been growing as a consequence. Our plans for the future were taking shape and we were looking forward to them – her dental projects completed and in operation, a little place of our own in retirement with the promise to continue to assist in any way possible.

But it was not to be. The answer was not clear to Susie nor is it to me at this point. In her illness, she hung on, hoping against hope, till the inevitable became clear. We sat down and planned her funeral together. 'I don't want a sad funeral,' she said characteristically. She deferred writing her will till the very last moment possible. We prayed, together and as a family, every day in hospital. The support we received from relatives and friends, both in Seychelles and from overseas, was beyond words.

Meanwhile, I am trying to learn more about the place of suffering in God's plan.

'Cast down but not destroyed'

One of the toughest things was to witness Susie undergo increasing suffering. It was as though there was a destructive force which was all out to destroy her physically and in every other way. However, there was an inner something (or Somebody?) in her, over which that adverse power did not prevail. In the end I prayed that the Lord would take her. Death came as her cure and relief!

Her closest friend, a member of the dental clinic staff, said afterwards: 'I was afraid of death until I sat with Susie through her illness and watched her die. I am not afraid any more. She has taught me how to die.'

There were a number of cancer patients who had got very close to Susie in their common treatment and need. To a non-Christian fellow patient and friend she said: 'I will be able to do more for all of you where I am going than I could ever do here.' Some of them have died since. They did not forget what she said.

Life's lessons

Places of learning and books teach us so much. However, there are certain lessons which only life itself can teach us. Frances, Michelle and I can now understand the bereavement of others in a way that we could not before Susie's passing. I now understand better the meaning of a 'wounded healer'.

We are deeply grateful for having been given the opportunity to contribute to this book. It has helped us to express our feelings in a way we had not done before. This has proved very therapeutic. Also, very importantly, Susie was sad she was not able to 'tell you everything' herself, as she had been anticipating. We are glad we have had the opportunity to try and do it on her behalf.

Her memory of Lambeth '88 remained vivid as one of the highlights of her life. Her wish was that this would prove true for the spouses attending the 1998 conference, especially those who will be coming for the first time.

The Bishop and I

Please accept this written contribution from our family as a token of our gratitude to God for the gift of Susie's life and all she will always mean to us and those who have known her.

Eileen Carey's Prayer

God our Creator,
> You fashioned the world and made us in your own image.

> Yet we have not looked after what you have given us properly and what we have is unequally shared with our brothers and sisters in many parts of your world.
> Many are starving and in my First World country we are careless and selfish with all the good things you have given us.

Lord, forgive us.

Jesus our Saviour,
> God the Father sent His only Son into the world to save us from our sins if we would be willing to accept Him into our lives.

> Many of our brothers and sisters are living as refugees, others are in war-torn lands, many without enough food and water and with only a makeshift shelter for protection. Without You, Lord, they would have nothing, but their faith in you gives them hope and strength.
> In my First World country we often forget the suffering of others.
> We live in our very comfortable homes and worship in very beautiful churches and we often turn our backs on those less fortunate.

Lord, forgive us.

Holy Spirit our Comforter,
> Sent into our world at the first Pentecost to be our guide and comforter.

Help all the contributors to this book wherever they live to rely on the power of the Holy Spirit in their lives.

Help us all to support one another in prayer and in any practical way we can as we all try in our own way to support our spouses in their calling as bishops in your Church.

In the name of the Father, the Son and the Holy Spirit. Amen